W9-CPV-285

what are you

hungry for?

also by mary taylor

New Vegetarian Classics: Soups
New Vegetarian Classics: Entrées
Lunch Crunch: Beating the Lunch Box Blues

lynn ginsburg

and mary taylor

illustrations by josef pusedu

ST. MARTIN'S PRESS ♠ NEW YORK

what are you

hungry for?

WOMEN, FOOD, AND SPIRITUALITY

WHAT ARE YOU HUNGRY FOR? WOMEN, FOOD, AND SPIRITUALITY.
Copyright © 2002 by Lynn Ginsburg and Mary Taylor. All rights
reserved. Printed in the United States of America. No part of this book
may be used or reproduced in any manner whatsoever without
written permission except in the case of brief quotations embodied in
critical articles or reviews. For information, address St. Martin's Press,
175 Fifth Avenue, New York, N.Y. 10010.

Illustrations © 2002 by Josef Pusedu

ISBN 0-312-26697-9

First Edition: January 2002

10 9 8 7 6 5 4 3 2 1

In loving memory of Carol Taylor and

Rachel Freeman for teaching me the

meaning of womanhood. M.T.

With all my love for Joe:

"The best is yet to be." L.G

contents

contents

x

acknowledgments

So many people have given us their patient support and genuine interest over the four-year process of writing this book that it's impossible to thank everyone by name. So this thanks is extended to all of you with our sincere gratitude. Your caring and interest kept us going.

There are some people we must thank in particular; without their help, this book would never have gone beyond the stage of our chatting away as we drank chai together. So let us start off by thanking those who made possible that beloved chai, without which we would never have had the alertness and sweet attitude to keep going: the inspired Tom Theobald, beekeeper at Niwot Honey Farm, and the makers of Eden Soy Extra Vanilla Soy Milk (not the "lite," it didn't work for us!).

Most important, we'd like to thank our families. First the men in our lives: Mary's husband, Richard Freeman, and their son, Gabriel, and Lynn's husband, Josef Pusedu, are now better educated about women, food, and spirituality than any man may ever wish to be. They've been good humored, insightful, and genuinely caring over the years. We love them! And special thanks to Joe for all of his hard work and artistic talent in creating the graphics for this book and for designing our Web site. Special thanks also to Richard for reviewing the yoga section of the book and helping both of us to understand this ancient art and philosophy. We'd also like to thank our parents—Mary's father, Frank Taylor, and Lynn's parents, Werner and Suzanne Heim—for their belief in our writing and this project.

We'd also like to thank our agent, Jane Dystel, for taking a chance on two "new guys on the block" and for her limitless patience, wisdom, keen grasp of the industry, and dead-on advice. We were always so grateful to have her in our corner. Miriam Goderich, vice president at Jane's agency, was the plucky initial reader of our proposal, very generously wading through our lengthy first drafts. Miriam was a paragon of patience and tact. Without both Jane and Miriam, this project would never have gotten off the ground.

acknowledgments

Our editor at St. Martin's, Elizabeth Beier, believed in this book from the very beginning. She showed insight into the issues, taking our raw ideas and helping them come to life. Her kindness and fortitude through the revision process was greatly appreciated. Michael Connor, assistant editor on the book, was always a wonderful additional help and a cheerful voice on the other end of the phone.

Michael Morales, Lynn's dear friend since childhood and a longtime book editor, helped us tremendously. At the beginning, Mike's advice and assistance was key in finding an agent. Throughout the four years, whenever we were confused about the publishing process, Mike was there with well-seasoned advice and a well-timed joke—always deeply appreciated. His tenure in the blue chair is clearly evidenced by his punditry!

We'd also like to thank Wendy Zerin, M.D., for her generous advice and for her suggestions and revisions on the Buddhist meditation sections of the book. We are grateful to Aadil B.A. Palkhivala, who sat around the kitchen table with us and with boundless enthusiasm and passion discussed the importance of finding meaning and pursuing dharma. His ideas were of great help in formulating the dharma section of our book.

Others who've helped enormously are Diane Farris, Diane Fassel, and Jeanie Manchester for reading early drafts of the book and providing useful feedback. Bill Goldman, who would have "bought stock" in us if only we'd have sold it—his enthusiasm and buoyant good humor helped us through. Spencer Beasley, who took the time to try to knock some learning into Lynn's head but can't be held responsible for her grammar. Tami Simon of Sounds True Productions provided generous support and networking. Thanks to Dan Finney for the acupuncture and Melanie Lancaster for the massages, both of which kept us up and running. We also thank Donna Fone, Rodney Yee, and John Robbins for their support and endorsement, and David and Helena Balduc, owners of the Boulder Bookstore, for their ongoing advice and knowledge of the book business.

We'd also like to thank Kathryn Arnold, Wynn Beardsley, Diane Botticelli, Teresa Bradford, Johanna Jongkind, Joanne Murphy, Lauren Piscopo, Tom Quinn, along with Jessica and Galen, Lois Sandusky, Erich Schiffmann, and Denise Snell. So many of our friends at the Yoga Workshop in Boulder displayed an enduring interest and support for our work, never tiring of asking "How's the book?" over the course of those four long years. This community has been our sangha and our refuge. Thank you all. And to all of the women who have attended our workshops, you've been inspirational!

In loving memory: Edith Beasley, Venable Herndon, Osita, Pen Wu, and Stitious. Your presence is with us!

preface

The problem that has no name—which is simply the fact that American women are kept from growing to their full human capacities—is taking a far greater toll on the physical and mental health of our country than any known disease.

—BETTY FRIEDAN, AUTHOR OF *THE FEMININE MYSTIQUE*

"You've come a long way, baby." We've all heard these words from the breezy advertising jingle, proclaiming the successes of the women's-lib movement. And look how far we've come: we modern women have attained such inalienable rights as the right to have a career, the right to vote, the right to serve our families fast-food takeout for dinner, and even the right to refuse to shave our legs. At last we've been freed from our indentured slavery as unpaid domestic servants. So, if women have come such a long way, why is it that we still feel utterly worthless if we're not slim and beautiful?

Wait a minute—who said we'd come such a "long way," anyway? The force behind that brash women's-lib slogan was actually the tobacco manufacturer Philip Morris. In 1968 they developed the "You've come a long way, baby" advertising campaign to launch the company's new line of cigarettes targeted at women smokers—Virginia Slims.

Apparently, our liberated status as women meant we were now free to court lung cancer along with the men, smoking our very own cigarette. But Virginia Slims weren't just any cigarette; they were designed to meet a woman's "special" needs. At last we had a cigarette "appropriate" for women—a skinny cigarette.

Yes, women have come a long way on some fronts. But we're still haunted by the specter of skinniness. Even as we make strides toward capturing greater economic and political power, there's a different story going on behind closed doors. We spend an astounding amount of money on the dieting industry—Americans alone spend upward of $33 billion each year trying to lose weight.*

*Mary K. Serdula, MD, MPH, et al., "Prevalence of Attempting Weight Loss and Strategies for Controlling Weight," *Journal of the American Medical Association* (JAMA), Vol. 282 (1999), 1353–58.

While proclaiming our liberation and maybe even burning a bra or two, we women still pour our hearts and incomes into the purchase of every new diet book, exercise gadget, scale, and miracle cellulite-reduction cream we can lay our hands on. Even though we may have come a long way, we're still victims of the paradox of our times—free to make our way in the world but prisoners of an age-old enslavement to our looks.

The two of us began working on this book as "liberated" women who understood the pain of this paradox all too well. We each had a secret that we'd never spoken aloud concerning our own past history with food and body issues. But eventually we started discussing the topic together, and once we did, we couldn't stop—finally we could share this intimate experience with someone else.

We were astonished to discover how much we had in common. The outward manifestations of our food and body conflicts seemed almost polar opposites. But our internal experience of the problem and the methods we'd found to resolve our issues were almost identical.

Lynn had been caught up in a cycle of yo-yo dieting since she was a teenager. Wanting to lose just a few pounds became a full-time obsession that took on a life of its own. Her focus on weight eventually became a self-fulfilling prophecy: with every diet she went on over the years, she had more and more weight to lose.

Dieting became an end game she couldn't possibly win, but she felt she couldn't possibly concede, either.

On the other end of the dieting spectrum, Mary became anorexic at the age of eighteen. Her struggle began when she was a freshman in college and had gained weight for the first time. She started dieting and lost the weight she'd gained. But within eight months, her "diet" had evolved into an all-out war against ever feeling her own hunger. As her weight became dangerously low, compliments on her weight loss stopped. By the middle of her sophomore year, she'd entered a realm of self-denial and deceit that left her weighing a mere seventy-five pounds—and still dieting.

While we were caught in our individual food and body crises, we were missing the deeper point. We so sincerely trusted a number on a scale, a dress size, or the omnipotent rightness of a measuring cup that we found ourselves believing our own self-worth was intrinsically tied to our appearance.

The impetus for resolving the food and body crisis came to each of us, oddly enough, in our sleep. It was as if the only place we could be totally honest with ourselves about how troubled we were was in our dreams.

At the low point of her anorexic episode, Mary dreamed that she sat up in bed and looked down to see her legs. To her shock, they had turned into the legs of a skeleton. In the dream, she reached down to touch the bones, and they collapsed into a pile of ashes. She woke up with a start, realizing that she'd reached a point where she must choose which direction she'd take—life or death. This certainly put her "dieting" in perspective, and she felt compelled to find something that had meaning beyond her struggle with food and her body.

Lynn's realization came one night at about four in the morning, when she woke suddenly from a deep sleep. In a flash of insight, she saw how much of her life she'd wasted playing a game with food and her looks. She realized it was no game, and that behaving this way had damaged her health and spirit. She felt she'd somehow lost her way, betraying herself. She could see that if she didn't make some profound changes and shift her priorities, she was going to waste her entire life obsessing about her body and other surface issues that were ultimately meaningless. She felt that her only choice was to either grow old, embittered, and unfulfilled, or to immediately stop treating her life as a game and focus on what really mattered.

As we worked on the book together and spoke about our past experiences with food and body, we were amazed that each of us had found our way out of crisis by reconnecting with our own true nature, recognizing after our wake-up call that we cared passionately about life. Not only did we care about our own existence, we both longed to connect to something that went beyond the realm of our own everyday experience. These insights had brought our lives around full circle: for the first time in years, we were feeling like ourselves again, as if we'd come home.

As we made changes in our lives, not every moment of every day was blissful and enlightened—far from it. But we did have a strong sense of purpose guiding us and helping us to make choices that brought us back to our ideals. That was satisfying in and of itself. We realized this sense of fulfillment was what we'd been hungry for all along.

This book has grown out of the insights that we both shared, out of our mutual conversations, and out of conversations we've had with other women who struggle with similar issues. We contend that, for so many women, the root cause of the food and body conflict is a void inside, a disconnect from the true self. When we buy into the illusion of beauty, we become blind to a more profound reality. Because we expend so much energy trying to sort out our endlessly complicated food and body issues, we never have enough of ourselves available to ponder questions like "Why am I alive?" "What is the ultimate meaning of our existence?" or "What lies beyond the mirror?"

This is one of the greatest sorrows of our time for women: that we can't even get on the path to pursue our true potential because we're so distracted by the torturous riddle of how to find happiness through achieving the perfect body. But this riddle is no more soluble than a Chinese finger puzzle—the more we thrash about to free ourselves, the more ensnared we become. Nonetheless, we somehow seem to retain an endlessly renewable optimism that someday we'll figure it all out and emerge victorious, gorgeous and perfectly fit. That's for someday, but in the meantime we're completely preoccupied while what really matters in life passes us by.

And there you have in a nutshell the entire paradox of women's so-called emancipation. No matter how far we've come, no matter what our achievements and accomplishments are, as women the ultimate measure of our success remains how good we look. That's the way it's always been, and that's the way it still is. As a woman you can be the peer of any man as long as you're beautiful and slim.

And that brings us back to those long, slim cigarettes. What body-conscious woman wouldn't embrace this declaration from Philip Morris's ad in 1971: "The makers of Virginia Slims feel it highly inappropriate that women continue to use the fat, stubby cigarettes designed for mere men . . . Virginia Slims, slimmer than the cigarettes men smoke."

In 1978, ten years after Virginia Slims congratulated women on their achievements, Susie Orbach questioned that feminine progress with her book *Fat Is a Feminist Issue.* Her thesis was that as long as beauty and slimness are our tickets to success, many women will choose to be unattractive and overweight as the only means of revolt against this oppressive system. She suggested that women must learn how to define beauty for themselves as a radical feminist act. While Orbach's message broke new ground on our path to discovering a deeper form of emancipation, we haven't come much further since her book's release.

It's time for a new manifesto and a new definition of beauty and liberation. We propose that the ultimate goal for women today is achieving true happiness, and that it doesn't come from surface fulfillment. Being allowed to wear pants, smoke skinny cigarettes, and challenge the men at their own game is simply not enough. If we're free on the outside while still trapped inside, believing that life is worthwhile only if we're slim and beautiful, then what's the point? Until women are free to be themselves—each a whole person with an inside and an outside—they will never feel truly liberated or truly beautiful.

This book will help you discover your own sense of meaning and spirituality so you can define your own beauty from the inside out. It will take you on a journey of self-discovery that can help you undo habits that keep you stuck in an imbalanced relationship with food and your body. You'll discover that liberation comes through true happiness, when you pursue whatever holds deeper meaning for *you*.

Each of us carries with us our own unique purpose, and our

own unique sense of what makes life meaningful. We can pursue a more meaningful existence. But the first step is leaning how to drop the "scales from our eyes," how to stop chasing a collective delusion of beauty that leads us ever further from happiness. Only then can you find a happiness that goes well beyond a number on a scale.

what are you

hungry for?

ONE

start where you are

Nor was I hungry; so I found
That hunger was a way
Of persons outside windows,
The entering takes away.

—EMILY DICKINSON, "I HAD BEEN HUNGRY"

the secret society of women

Women have many secrets. But our secret relationship with food and our body can come to overshadow all other aspects of life, filling us with obsession, shame, and fear. This relationship is intense and intimate, and the compulsion to maintain the secret can become the driving force behind everything we do and think. On the surface we may appear sane, but inside we're engaged in a never-ending tug-of-war.

We're writing this book because we personally know the debilitating cost, both physical and emotional, of keeping your relationship to food and your body a secret. We know how it is to always feel the struggle with food lurking just below the surface. We've put in more time than we care to remember on berating our looks and trying to be anyone other than who we are.

When your relationship with food and your body feels this out of control, getting through the day can be like scurrying through a minefield. You feel that no matter which way you turn, something is going to blow up in your face. You cheat on your diet, you're horrified by your reflection in the mirror, a button pops on your pants. At the end of the day, you're filled with regret and self-hatred once again. This inner turmoil takes its toll. It saps our vital energies and keeps us from what we really want to do with our lives.

But our personal experience has also shown us that this struggle with food and body can become a catalyst for change. It can force us to connect to life on the deepest level.

When we're ready to make a deep and pervasive change, our struggle with food and body can serve as a wake-up call. The pain we feel can motivate us to learn how to nourish our deepest self. This book starts from that deep place of motivation. It's intended to serve as your guide through resolving your inner battle.

the food and body conflict

For many women, a sense that life is good, that we're valuable and accomplished, is often directly tied into how we look. So many of us spend countless years dreaming about the good old days when we could eat anything, or holding out for that mirage of a slender body glimmering just ahead on the horizon.

Why we believe that life is worthwhile only if we look good can be traced to a variety of factors. Cultural standards and pressures, messages from the media, the warped feminine psyche that emerges in a patriarchal society, a striving for perfection, and competitiveness with other women are among the many components that contribute.

Whatever the reasons, the message is clear: women in our society must be thin to be valued. We put unrelenting pressure on ourselves to "effortlessly" maintain a contrived look. We're not rewarded for nurturing an individual appearance. Instead, we try to shape our appearance to fit the fashion template of the day. We

don't win by being who we are *now*. The result is that we find ourselves embroiled in a ceaseless food and body conflict.

The *food and body conflict* is a relationship with food and body
that dominates our thoughts and actions to the point of debilitating our lives. We feel pain and shame, and we don't know how to
break free of the conflict. It affects every aspect of our lives, color-
ing our decisions, relationships, and ability to function in a healthy
way.

Millions of American women spend huge amounts of energy,
time, and money on a pilgrimage to an illusion of beauty. On any
given day, 40 percent of all American women are actively dieting.[*]
Another five to ten million women apparently suffer from the eating disorders of anorexia, bulimia, and compulsive overeating, the
extreme forms of food and body conflicts.[†] But equally depleting
are the more subtle forms of the conflict. Not so easily categorized
are the demoralizing ups and downs of yo-yo dieting, ongoing
low-grade starvation, or a rigid exercise regime.

Whatever the conflict looks like on the outside, most women
experience remarkably similar feelings on the inside. First and fore-
most is suffering. We suffer over what seem to be unresolvable be-

[*]"Methods of Voluntary Weight Loss and Control," National Institutes of Health
Technology Assessment Conference Statement, March 30–April 1, 1992.
[†]The Web site of Eating Disorders Awareness and Prevention, Inc. (EDAP): www.
edap.org/edinfo/stats.html.

4

haviors and thinking traps. We feel stuck in a battle between what we long for our bodies to look like and what we see in the mirror. We struggle over what to eat, when to eat, how to exercise, and what diet to follow this time. We suffer when the diet doesn't work, when willpower fails, when destructive patterns of thought and behavior prevail, and when attaining our ideal appearance slips impossibly out of reach—again.

Accompanying this underlying sense of suffering is a feeling of emptiness. We feel something missing. Inside of us is a void, a longing deep within for some elusive satisfaction. This empty feeling is often experienced physically as gnawing hunger, as if we have a bottomless hole inside. If we're to fill this void, we must start by asking: what is the source of this feeling of emptiness? For so many women, it's a longing for spiritual fulfillment that leaves us always hungry and dissatisfied.

We define *spirituality* as a belief in that which goes beyond our material, corporeal existence, giving us faith that there's more to life than the everyday experience. Spirituality is a faith in God, Nature, a higher consciousness, or any other power greater than our singular mortal existence.

When we've lost a spiritual connection in our lives, we may eat and eat in an attempt to fill our inner void. But satisfaction comes only when we're able to rediscover our connection to whatever holds deepest meaning for us.

5

west meets east

For women living in the Western world, finding and maintaining a spiritual connection can be difficult. In the West, religion and spirituality typically get relegated to Sundays, holidays, and crises. According to a 1997 Gallup poll on spiritual beliefs, the number of Americans who believe that religion has lost its influence on American life has increased from 3 percent in the 1950s to a staggering 60 percent in 1997. Yet 82 percent of Americans say they're conscious of the presence of God; 57 percent report having had an important religious experience; and 36 percent say they've had a mystical experience. We're a society hungry for spirituality, but we aren't finding it within our daily lives. Without it, our search for fulfillment focuses purely on the material realm. This leaves many Western women looking for deeper meaning.

The ideas and solutions presented in this book are inspired by Eastern healing and spiritual practices. What differentiates the Eastern approach is a long, unbroken tradition of seeking fulfillment through the practice of internal contemplation. According to Eastern philosophy, the internal world is our entry into a spiritual existence where we find meaning beyond our corporeal lives. Meditation, concentrated prayer, and other deep states of consciousness are examples of actively connecting to our internal spiritual realm.

The Eastern approach takes into account both internal and external existence. It embraces the individual as a whole being. From this perspective, when a person has a problem that manifests on the outside (a symptom), there is a corresponding cause on the inside.

According to the Eastern approach, you must treat the internal root cause to heal an external symptom. If you simply eliminate the symptom, the fundamental issues that caused the problem remain. Sooner or later they'll resurface.

Traditional Western diets fail to resolve the food and body conflict because they don't deal with the root cause. They try to cure the external symptom of being overweight with a low-calorie diet. They counter bulimia with Prozac. They curtail overeating with an appetite suppressant. External solutions like these can provide quick relief and may succeed for a short time. But eventually they fail because they haven't treated the root cause.

Rudyard Kipling said long ago, "East is East, and West is West, and never the twain shall meet." But time-tested Eastern healing practices are just the solution to our modern Western-style food and body conflict. By blending the wisdom of both cultures, we can learn to heal. We can be women in Western society who find life worthwhile not because we're thin but because it's filled with meaning.

what are you doing *right now*?

When we don't find meaning in our present circumstances, we're haunted by ghosts of the past and fantasies of the future. We're punished by thoughts of our past, such as "Why did I eat all of that cake last night?" or "Why can't I look as thin as I did last summer?" Turning from the past, we focus on the future. We try to comfort ourselves with plans like "Tomorrow I'll follow my diet strictly" or "Two months from now, I'll be down to my ideal weight."

But this book starts you off in the present moment. Whatever your own personal history with dieting, it's in the past. Whatever your hopes for the future, they'll forever remain just that—aspirations, fervent prayers. By coming to know yourself in the present, you can start to find peace with food and your body right now.

To help you start healing, this book offers practices that teach you how to focus on the here and now. Many of these practices are designed for you to return to again and again. You'll need a notebook or journal where you can keep your notes for the practices.

how to get the most out of the practices: These practices will help you understand and resolve the complex workings of your own food and body conflict. As you read through the book, you may find it helpful to stop and do the practices along the way. Or you may find it more useful to first read all the way through the book without stopping. If you take this approach, you can envision the practices in your mind as you read along. Once you've gotten the bigger picture of the book, then you can go back and complete the practices.

A note of caution: One of the greatest blocks to resolving food and body issues can be a stifling perfectionism that keeps us stuck. Don't let the feeling that you must do the practices perfectly keep you from finishing the book and understanding the complete path to resolving your food and body conflict.

PRACTICE: WAKING UP

Right now, in this present moment, maybe your back is aching, you're hungry, your mind is wandering, you're thinking of the errands you have to run. Dig a little deeper and you might realize that you're feeling sad and regretful about a conversation you had with your spouse this morning. Or perhaps you're anxious about unfinished work at the office. Or you may be excitedly anticipating your dinner with friends this evening. Whatever the content of *your* thoughts, *your* feelings, *your* physical sensations, that's what's real for you right now.

1. Begin this practice by finding a comfortable place where you can sit uninterrupted for five minutes. Have a clock or watch,

your journal, and a pen nearby. Sit with your back straight
and your head held evenly.

2. Note in your journal what time it is as you begin.

3. Now close your eyes. Simply observe everything that wanders through your mind. You may have a series of thoughts,
or you may become aware of sounds or sensations. Whatever
presents itself is your experience of the present moment.

4. The first time you feel compelled to check the time, make
note of how long you've been sitting: thirty seconds, one
minute, or five minutes. There's no right or wrong amount
of time.

5. Write down how long you sat before you checked the time.
Also note whatever went through your mind while sitting.

6. Now try a different variation of the sitting practice. This
time, before you begin, focus your mind for a moment on
food and your body.

7. Again close your eyes and observe everything you experience
as you sit. Make special note of anything that comes into your
mind that relates to food and how you feel about your body.

8. Make note if you're able to sit longer without checking the
time.

Reflection: Every moment of every day of your life, you have
a stream of thoughts and sensations that flows through your

awareness. This seemingly mundane stream is what makes up *your* reality.

What you've just recorded in your journal is a snapshot of your day-to-day experience of the present moment. As you repeat this practice, you may notice that you can spend more time observing your current reality. It's from this space of the present moment that you'll gradually begin to heal your food and body conflict.

PRACTICE: WHAT'S YOUR PROBLEM?

What motivated you to pick up this book? What's bothering you about food and your body? What changes would you like to make in your life?

It's now time to identify what you personally perceive as your *problem* and what you want to do about it. This desire for change is your *intention.*

1. Set aside five to ten minutes for this practice. Sit comfortably, and clear your mind: breathe slowly and rhythmically and start tuning into the sound of your breath. As thoughts, feelings, and physical sensations arise, take a deep breath in. As you breathe out, release the thought, feeling, or physical sensation with the outgoing breath.

11

2. Now contemplate your personal experience of the food and body conflict. Observe the thoughts that arise about food and body: your behaviors, eating patterns, and feelings about your body.

3. When you open your eyes, think about all that's traveled in and out of your awareness in the past few minutes. Out of everything that's occurred to you, what seems to be the greatest problem? What's the most important thing you want to change about your relationship to food and your body?

4. Now write down what you see as your food and body problem and what you want to change—your intention. Try to state each in a single sentence. For instance, you might say, "My problem is that I'm thirty pounds overweight. My intention is that I want to lose thirty pounds." Or you could be experiencing a more elusive problem: "My problem is that I'm totally confused about how to eat in a relaxed and healthy way. My intention is that I want to learn how to relate to food normally."

5. In your journal, record the results from this practice as your starting point—your beginning problem and intention. In future practices, you'll be asked to refer back to your problem and intention.

Reflection: As you begin to heal your food and body conflict, you may discover that your original problem and intention don't match your current circumstances. If so, return to this practice to check in with how you're currently experiencing your problem and intention. Then restate them to match your current circumstances.

the practice of healing

Growing up in Western society, we're programmed to believe that every problem has a quick and easy solution. Have a headache? Take an aspirin. Coughing? Take a cough suppressant. Feel overweight? Go on a diet. Problem solved!

As you begin the process of healing your food and body conflict, you may find yourself wanting a quick resolution. Most of us who have dieted before are looking for that quick fix, like the Slim-Fast slogan: "Give us a week, and we'll take off the weight."

But we can cure the problem for a week only to have it return the next. If you were to tune back in the week after you "took off the weight," you'd probably find that you gained it all back—plus a few extra pounds as a bonus. The quick fix that we're promised for instant salvation never seems to last. To find change that endures, you have to heal your food and body conflict at its roots.

TWO

are you looking at yourself from the outside in?

"And if you're not good directly," she added, "I'll put you through into Looking-glass House. How would you like that?"

—LEWIS CARROLL, ALICE FROM *THROUGH THE LOOKING GLASS*

mirror, mirror . . .

Every day, before we go out into the world, we enact a daily ritual of stepping before the mirror. Sometimes with hesitation, sometimes with hope, we come face-to-face with the reflection. Like

Snow White's wicked stepmother, we consult the oracle of the mirror, asking, "Mirror mirror on the wall, who's the fairest of them all?"

Most of us don't expect the mirror to tell us we're the fairest. But nonetheless, every day we ask this shiny reflective surface to assess our beauty. And we trust it to tell us the truth.

It's easy to look at your reflection and create a distorted picture of who you are. For many of us, the mirror becomes our most trusted confidant and our most stern confessor. Only it sees our stomach muscles completely relaxed and our nose hairs before they're removed. The mirror is like the priest at confession to whom we reveal our true selves—from sags and bags to stretch marks and wrinkles.

Much of what we know about ourselves is based on what we see. But we can't *actually* see ourselves. We can't see our whole bodies, except in a mirror, a shop window, a photo, or a video. We rely on these reflected images to tell us who we are. But even with these images, we're still not getting the whole picture. There's no mirror, shop window, photo, or video that can show you who you are on the inside.

But as we stare at the image in the mirror, we become firmly convinced that what we see is who we really are. This illusion that we're nothing more than an image can ruin our lives. What happens to our internal existence if we're only a picture or a reflection?

who's that in the mirror?

Sharon had recently gained twenty-five pounds. Having never gained appreciable amounts of weight before, she felt deeply ashamed of her appearance.

Sharon began to obsessively stare at herself in every reflective surface she could find. From mirrors and windows to oven doors and blank television screens, wherever Sharon looked, her image stared back menacingly. She felt surrounded by all the reminders of the disgusting blob she'd become.

One day Sharon went to lunch at a Chinese restaurant with some friends. With a sense of righteous deprivation, she ordered the healthy special (steamed vegetables and chicken with low-sodium soy sauce on the side). As the background conversation droned on, Sharon stared at the reflection of her face in the stainless-steel teapot. With distress, she saw puffy round cheeks that spread out almost past her ears, and squinty little eyes topped by a Neanderthal-looking forehead. "There I am," she thought, "as glamorous as ever."

That thought snapped Sharon out of her reverie for just a moment. She realized that her image was being distorted by the curvature of the teapot. She'd been berating herself about a reflection that was no more accurate than a fun-house mirror.

This realization gave Sharon the insight that her obsession with her image was a much greater problem than her weight gain. She had somehow lost sight of herself as a whole person, thinking of herself only as a fat blob who'd gained twenty-five pounds. She had come to believe that her reflection was the sum total of who she was. After seeing herself in the teapot, she understood that her image was just a tiny piece of her. In order to really see herself, she now knew that she needed to take into account her whole being—outside and inside.

PRACTICE: LOOKING INTO THE MIRROR

This practice is similar to the sitting practice introduced in the previous chapter, where you noted your thoughts as you sat with your eyes closed. But this time you'll be standing in front of a mirror with your eyes open.

part one

1. Go to a full-length mirror. Before you step in front of it, set a goal to just look at your reflection objectively. Then step before the mirror.
2. As you gaze at yourself, become conscious of what you see.
3. When you notice that your mind has wandered and you're

no longer specifically observing your reflection, step away from the mirror.

4. In your journal, describe in detail how you saw your reflection—"curved shapes," "stubby arms," "stringy hair," et cetera. Also record any thoughts, feelings, and sensations that contemplating your body provokes.

5. Write down any negative conclusions you made about yourself as a whole person based on your reflection: "I am a fat pig" or "I hate myself."

6. Also make note of whatever part of your body you looked at first: your hips, your wrinkles, the blemish on your forehead.

7. Over the course of the next several days, repeat this practice. Try to slow down the observation process and experience as much detail as possible.

part two

Once you've completed Part One, you can make the conscious effort to shift your perspective. This will help to break the patterns with which you perceive yourself.

1. Before you step in front of the mirror, think about the part of your body that you always focus on first. Also consider how your dislike of your body translates to conclusions about yourself as a whole person.

2. Make the conscious decision not to look at the parts of your body that you typically focus on first. Instead, choose a part of your body that you either feel neutral about or like (such as your eyes or hands).

3. Now step in front of the mirror. Look immediately at the part of your body that you'd chosen.

4. Gradually broaden your gaze to encompass a more whole view of your body. Notice if this interrupts your pattern of self-judgment.

Reflection: By continuing to observe your reflection over time, you'll notice that what you see changes from day to day and even from hour to hour. You've got the same body—but your mood, how you're feeling physically, or a compliment you've received can completely alter your perception of what you see.

It's important to realize that your *perception* is completely subjective and temporary. On a bad day, you may believe that what you see in the mirror is real and unalterable. But watching how your reflection changes over time can prove that's not true.

When we perceive ourselves as nothing more than a picture, we suffer because we lose sight of our inner selves. We may know logically that basing our self-worth solely on our body's reflection in a mirror is ridiculous. But practically, it can prove almost impossible to stop such a deeply ingrained pattern of judging ourselves.

Bringing conscious awareness to the ritual of looking at ourselves in the mirror can break our patterned ways of seeing. When we make the conscious effort to stop basing self-worth on an image, we can see that we're much more than a reflection in a mirror.

the covenant

In our society, a woman's value is often equated with how she looks. As women, we're programmed to value our appearance as one of the most important aspects of our self-worth. But men have also been programmed to respond to a woman's external image.

Walk down the street with an average friend and you may get polite nods or furtive glances from men. If you make the same journey with a tall friend who has long, sweeping blond hair or a buxom companion sporting a snugly stretched sweater, men stop and stare. No matter how liberated we are, we're still judged by our appearance.

Our initial response might be to place all the blame on the men who—almost as a reflex—tune into a "babe." But far more insidious and destructive is the way women value other women according to appearance. We may intellectually know that beauty is only skin-deep, but on some subconscious level, the message is passed on from mother to daughter, woman to woman, that looks are paramount. This is deeply ingrained in all of us from a young age: a 1999 Exeter University survey of girls aged twelve to fifteen showed 57.5 percent considered their appearance to be the biggest concern in their lives.

It's as though women have a confidential, unspoken social contract that looks count above all. In this book, we call this unspoken social contract between women *the Covenant*. If you've ever been on a diet, ever judged another woman by her appearance, or ever compared yourself to a model in a magazine, then you're an active participant in the Covenant.

This isn't to say that looking beautiful isn't something to enjoy. Indeed, appealing to yourself is vital to good health and well-being. But when you lose sight of what holds meaning for you and instead focus on your appearance, then the Covenant is destructive.

When we're tired of making the effort to be someone we're not, then maybe we've finally had enough. If you decide that you'll no longer allow your outer appearance to define you as a human being, then you're ready to break the Covenant.

What happens when you decide to break the Covenant? How about all of the other people who still continue to apply its standards to you? You may be through with the Covenant, but it's not through with you. Heading out on your own and going against the tide of society can be intimidating. You may experience a sense of

fear and foreboding at the prospect. But then it starts to sink in—
what a relief, to be free of that trap!

When you decide to break the Covenant, you'll find something
subtle and powerful taking place inside you. You start to wake up.
You realize that you've spent so much time focused on food and
your body that it's absorbed years of your life.

While you were counting calories and weighing yourself, the
real drama of your life was being played out on another stage. Stop
for a moment and estimate roughly how much time over the years
you've spent thinking or obsessing about food and your body. Consider the great things you might have accomplished with that
same amount of time and energy. What you've been missing out
on is really living life, pursuing what's most meaningful to you as
an individual. When you're no longer following the dictates of the
Covenant, you'll finally have the opportunity to discover your
own meaning.

trespassing

By trying to change yourself to match the ideals of the Covenant,
you suffer deeply. When you try to be someone you're not, you be-
tray your own truths in service of those that come from outside.

When you cross that line of authenticity within, knowingly going against your most deeply held beliefs and values, you trespass against yourself. We're taught to acknowledge and forgive trespasses—both trespasses that others have committed against us and the trespasses that we commit against others.

But how about the trespasses that we commit against ourselves? When we trample on our own essence, the damage lies within and is typically invisible to the outside world. It's worse than someone else forcing you to do something you don't want to do or don't believe in—you've gone against your own gut sense of right and wrong.

This feeling of self-betrayal is all too familiar for women with a food and body conflict. We reject who we actually are in favor of a "new," "improved," "much better" self. Our own values and standards get squelched in favor of the "superior" values of the Covenant. When we do this, we inevitably trespass against ourselves.

there's more to the picture than meets the eye

When you judge yourself based on your external appearance, you become a prisoner of the belief that you're no more than your body. A far deeper reality exists for all of us beneath the surface. That reality is who we are on a soulful, spiritual level: our internal sense of what is true, meaningful, and unchanging. Learning to connect to this deeper reality is a key factor in resolving any food and body conflict.

It's natural to identify with your body. It's the boundary between you and the rest of the world, the package of yourself that others see. Because your body is the part of you that interfaces with the rest of the world, and because it has such dominant needs— you have to wash it, feed it, burp it, and so on—it is, in some ways, the most concrete thing you deal with on a daily basis. It can therefore become the overwhelming focal point for your sense of self.

But you *are* much more than your body. There's no more striking proof of this than the simple fact that after a person dies, his or her body remains, but the person is clearly gone. Who was here, and who is gone after death?

The mirror can actually be your ally in coming to understand that you are much more than your body. By watching your physical form evolve over time, you realize that this external image isn't permanent. Sometimes the mirror shows us things we like, and sometimes it doesn't, but it's only a day-to-day snapshot of our outside. As you look at this outside view, ask yourself, "Who is it inside who's looking out?"

through the looking glass (and what alice found there)

Just as Alice stepped through the mirror and discovered a wondrous hidden world, there's an unseen land that lies hidden within each of us. But there's no mirror that can bounce back the reflection of your inner landscape, with its complex thoughts, emotions, sensations, perceptions, and memories.

Just as it's frightening to step into an unknown patch of woods in the night when you have no idea what may be lurking, so we can be terrified of stepping within ourselves and finding what lies inside. In some ways, our exterior seems safer. We think if we can control our outer appearance, than we have control over ourselves, our lives, and our destinies.

But we are beings with an inside *and* an outside. For most women who are caught up in a food and body conflict, their inside is calling the shots. When we feel desperately unhappy with our appearance and our lives, that's coming from the inside.

When our sense of self comes from our external appearance, we focus on fixing up the outside. We keep incredibly busy counting calories, exercising, and weighing ourselves in an ongoing attempt to renovate our appearance. But satisfaction seems to elude us. Somehow we can never fill the emptiness inside, the void. We have a nagging feeling that something fundamental is missing in our lives.

Alice was an adventurer, a girl driven by an exquisite sense of curiosity to discover the unknown. She felt compelled to go into the unexplored world, to find out what lay on the other side of the mirror. To heal ourselves, we, too, need to find a way to go inside and make our own journey of self-discovery. The path into that hidden world may feel fraught with danger. But even though exploration of the unknown carries risks, it can also provide the greatest reward: the answer to the questions "Who am I? Am I something beyond what I see in the mirror?"

THREE

turning yourself inside out

It is only with the heart that one can see rightly; what is essential is invisible to the eye.

—ANTOINE DE SAINT-EXUPÉRY, *THE LITTLE PRINCE*

what's in there?

If you've ever had the experience of snorkeling up to the edge of a freshwater spring, it can be quite a jolt. Swimming peacefully along, you become used to the subtle dips and curves in the bottom of the pool, and the gentle sway of the plant life. Suddenly you come to the mouth of the spring and swim out over the edge of a hundred-foot drop-off. Even though you're still floating on top of the water, moving over that edge can produce a terrifying illusion. You feel as if you're going to plummet down into the churning bottom of the spring and get sucked into the belly of the earth.

For many women, the thought of looking inside themselves can be equally frightening. But if you can cross over that moment of fear, you'll find that there's no danger of destroying yourself. Instead, just as the mouth of a spring reveals new depths of beauty, so looking into your inner self will offer you an experience of a deeper realm of life.

In Western society, we often think of this internal realm as the domain of psychologists. When women talk about the cause of their food and body conflict, the conversation can shift to psychological evaluations. Some women tell stories about how their mother or sisters criticized their looks, competed with them, ignored them, or formed a bond of dieting and calorie-counting. Others make the association between food and body problems and a struggle with perfectionism, relationships with men, or any number of other important psychological factors that have shaped their lives.

Recognizing the psychological basis that can drive us to eat and starve ourselves is an important step in resolving our food and body conflict. The psychological issues—the mental and emotional factors—that surround our perception of our body and our relationship with food are extremely significant. Working with a reputable therapist to understand the psychological issues that keep you stuck in your food and body conflict is a process we consider vital.

In this book, we explore the internal realm using Eastern practices, which integrate mind, body, and emotions. But Western therapy and Eastern mind/body practices are complementary. Pursuing both simultaneously can make each process more productive. With the help of a therapist, you can learn to examine actions and emotional states using your capacity for rational thought and reason. Through mind/body practices, you can learn to still the mind, observe the emotions, and listen to the messages your body presents. Combining the two approaches gives you the best of both worlds. East meets West once again.

deep-down happiness

On the surface, Michelle didn't seem to have any problems with food or her body. She was of average weight and attractive. But Michelle was hiding a secret inside. For years she'd suffered from intermittent binge/purge cycles in which she gorged herself, then used laxatives, forced herself to vomit, or starved herself for a few days to "make up" for the extra calories.

Michelle went for nutritional counseling, hoping to find a way out of these painful cycles. During the course of her therapy, one of her exercises was to draw her vision of what she looked like inside. At first she imagined a rather amorphous shape. As she continued drawing, she constructed a series of interlocking pieces that looked rather like countries on a map. She identified these pieces as the fragments of her life—her musical passion, doubts about her looks, her job, relationships, and so on.

When she returned to the drawing a week later, she saw that none of the shapes represented her secret behavior of binge eating. Although her goal in counseling was to work through his behavior, she realized that she was still hiding her secret because it was too painful for her to admit who she really was. She knew that to get past this problem, she had to face herself as she was right now.

She saw that her original tidy drawing showed just a surface-level veneer of herself. In order to see more deeply into her problem, she closed her eyes and started to visualize what a drawing of her binge/purge behavior might look like. She saw in her mind's eyes a huge throbbing shape that seemed to represent everything inside of her. It felt like a cloth bag packed full of worms, alive and wriggling with motion. As she contemplated this bag, it suddenly burst into a hideous picture of a giant sewer littered with rotting garbage and teeming with rats, clawing at the top to get out.

Michelle felt repulsed and frightened by this image. But knowing the sewer had arisen as she contemplated her eating behavior, she felt compelled to look at it more closely. Summoning her courage, she imagined ripping off the lid and looking at the teeming cesspool below.

She expected to be overwhelmed by the rankness and the onslaught of rats. Instead, when she imagined lifting off the lid, the seething sewer that she'd envisioned inside of her became still and shriveled away to nothing. She felt it was almost comical: what she'd feared would be a gruesome internal confrontation actually turned out to be a non-event. For the first time, she'd faced her secret eating behavior and felt an overwhelming sense of relief.

Michelle knew that she still had important work to do to resolve her binging and purging behavior. But by lifting off the lid of her imagined internal sewer, Michelle had taken the first step toward healing her food and body conflict: seeing herself as she *really* was, not as she feared she was.

going home

The poet T. S. Eliot stated quite simply, "Home is where one starts from." Though we may be eager to race forward into the future, where all our current problems will finally be happily resolved, here—right now—is where we must start from. Who you are to-day, inside *and* outside, is your home, your starting place.

The problem for most of us is that we find our "now" so un-bearable: because we feel out of control with our eating, because we're overweight, because our bodies just won't conform to our ideals. What keeps us stuck is trying to start from where we are not, instead of where we are.

We are not in the past or the future. We are here, right now, em-broiled in all of the current circumstances that make up our lives—our relationships with spouse, children, family, friends; our careers; our finances; our emotions; our predilections; our genet-ics; our personal history; our bodies as they are today. All of these circumstances constitute home base for each of us. They exist to-day, and are what we must work with if we want to make tomor-row's changes.

Say, for example, you hate how you look today because you're overweight. If you go on the most strict and Spartan diet, perhaps within a month you could start to change how you look. But even in the very fastest dieting scenario, what you're punishing yourself for today can't possibly be remedied tomorrow.

The one thing you *can* change immediately is your perspective. There comes a point in all of our lives when it's time to stop per-petually putting off happiness until some future date when everything will finally be in order. Right now, at this very moment as you read these words, you have an opportunity for happiness. There's no more powerful force for truly changing your life in the future than learning how to be happy today, as you are, at home in your body.

PRACTICE: ARE YOU HAPPY?

How often have you thought to yourself, "If only I could stop obsessing about food and lose those twenty pounds, I'd be so happy"? Whether it's something as seemingly superficial as fitting into a treasured size 4 dress, or a life-changing event such as resolving anorexic behaviors or finding a mate, many women feel as though their lives would be happy "if only."

1. Take a moment to consider your life as it is today. Do you feel *completely* happy with the way things are? If your answer is no, write down in your journal what you think would make you truly happy. Name anything and everything you think might remedy your situation: physical changes (a flatter stomach, trimmer hips, or smaller breasts), material improvements (a new car or bigger house), life transformations (a fulfilling job or relationship), or completely whimsical

fantasies (being a supermodel, winning the lottery). Write down whatever comes to mind.

2. Reorganize and rank this list according to what feels the most important for resolving your food and body conflict.

3. Work with the top three items from your list. Consider these selected items one by one, imagining that each has become fulfilled, that your wish has been granted and has become a very real and vital part of your life. Create detail about how having it come true would transform your life. Allow your mind to go wild with imagination as you bask in having your wish for happiness fulfilled.

4. Before moving on to the next step, make sure you've allowed yourself to imagine everything about this wish that could possibly make you happy.

5. When your imagined vision is as complete as possible, ask yourself again, "With all of this in place, am I now completely and totally happy? Is there anything more that I still want?"

6. If there's still something missing, quiet your mind and ask again what would make you happy. Do this again and again, searching your mind, heart, and soul for answers.

Reflection: As you work your way through this exercise, you'll probably find that you have a broad range of desires. You may start

your list for happiness by identifying what's most immediately distressing, such as wanting thin thighs. But as you fulfill (in your
imagination) your more surface-level wishes, you'll start tapping
into your deeper desires.

When you live out your fantasy of what you think will bring
you eternal happiness (flatter stomach, for example), you often
find that having your desire granted isn't the magical cure you've
long been dreaming of.

what is happiness? where does happiness come from?

Ask yourself a deceptively simple question: why have you been going to all of this effort to change your looks and your relationship
to food? The simplest answer cuts right to the heart of the matter—to be happy.

We want to make changes because we want to be happier. The
desire for happiness is one of the strongest motivating factors in
anyone's life. Denying ourselves basic happiness comes at the very
greatest cost to our well-being.

Happiness can work for or against you. Wanting something you
can't have makes you unhappy. But getting things you want
doesn't always make you happy. You think, "Oh, if I just had those

fabulous shoes in the window, I'd be so happy, I just know it."
Months later, as the shoes gather dust in the closet, your restless
need for happiness fixes on a new object of desire, and another, and
another.

On the other hand, when what you want is exactly what you
truly need, it can inspire you to go beyond what you may think
possible. For instance, you might determine that it would make
you happy to return to school and get an advanced degree in a subject you truly love. Your desire to fulfill this wish for happiness can
motivate you to accomplish the difficult work of getting your degree. You might not be deliriously happy every moment of every
day as you pursue your goal, but you'll feel a sense of fulfilling happiness on a deeper inner level.

We often believe that getting the objects we desire—such as
possessions, relationships, and ideas—will make us happy. Some of
these things grant immediate pleasure or satisfaction, such as a
flattering reflection in a mirror, a double-fudge chocolate brownie,
or the relief of feeling healthy after having the flu. But when we
leave the mirror, eat the brownie, or find our sniffles coming back,
the satisfaction disappears. If our happiness is dependent on anything that's transitory, we must always search for new things to
keep us happy.

For all of us, there's another form of happiness that isn't transitory; it is instead sustaining and renewing. It's the happiness we find when we're aligned with whatever it is in life that we find personally fulfilling and meaningful. Although other people, possessions, or thoughts can be part of it, they are never the origin of this deeper form of internal happiness. Internally rooted happiness simply *is*.

For women with a food and body conflict, believing that happiness is dependent on appearance can be the source of great unhappiness. The thin legs, shapely figure, or men's approving glances become what we seek to make us happy. When you've spent your entire life buying into the Covenant—that looks count above all else—you can come to believe that looking good is happiness personified.

If we accept society's Covenant that all good things come to those who look good, then of course we believe that looking good is happiness itself. All of life's joy clearly will follow if you can be the winner in the supermodel sweepstakes. But as you may have experienced in the "Are You Happy?" practice (see page 33), things that seem so desirable—like a thinner body or five more inches to your height—don't provide ultimate fulfillment.

The truth is that inside most women, there's a small voice that may get amplified when we're finally fed up: it says that we *do* want much more out of life than just to look good. If, at the end of our lives, we were to sum up our crowning achievement as "I was quite thin," that would not be enough.

Pursuing the myth that looks count above all else does not bring us happiness. Therefore it's time for us to form a new Covenant as women. We need to create dialogue and say openly to one another that lasting happiness doesn't come by simply being thin and looking fashionable. True happiness comes by leading a meaningful life that fills the void within—as each of us *individually* defines that meaning, not as others define it for us.

But how can we tap into finding what gives life meaning—not just anyone's life, but *your* life?

the meaning of dharma

The concept of leading a life with purpose and meaning is central to Hindu philosophy: it is called **dharma**. Dharma has many meanings within this philosophy, including justice, natural law, duty, righteousness, moral principles, that which holds everything together, and being true to one's inner nature. Buddhist thought refers to dharma in a similar manner, and Chinese philosophy has a parallel concept called the Tao (pronounced "dow").

In all of these ancient Eastern systems of thought, each of us has an intrinsically unique purpose—or dharma—at any given moment, and for our life as a whole. It's believed that finding and following your individual dharma is your duty and the ultimate purpose of every human life.

Dharma can be defined for individuals as one's inner nature and spiritual core. Actions and beliefs that are right for one person may be wrong for someone else. My dharma might be to use my talent for art to paint, whereas your dharma might be to use your talent for trading merchandise to be a businesswoman.

At the same time, our personal dharma can't be separated from the context of our lives as a whole. Eastern philosophies emphasize that to act appropriately according to our dharma, it's not enough to pursue our inner nature with disregard for everything else. Dharma is about responsibility to your own inner nature, and to the circumstances of your personal life.

Dharma reflects not only our own personal purpose but also how we pursue meaning within the circumstances of our lives as they are right now. It's the intricate relationship of who we are as individuals, combined with who we are as a part of the world in its entirety.

According to traditional Eastern thought, to go against one's dharma is wrong because it opposes our own personal nature and our rightful place in the world. If my talent and greatest love in life is art, and I pursue a business career rather than making any use of this talent, then I've gone against my personal dharma. But I'm also not following my dharma if I pursue my art at the expense of my responsibilities to family and other circumstances of my life.

Dharma can be considered as that which gives our lives meaning, our personal purpose for being. But living a life directed by this inner sense of meaning can be trying in a society that focuses on the external world.

Leading a fulfilling, meaningful life can be especially challenging for women. In so many ways, Western women have more freedom now than ever before in recorded history. We're better equipped to choose our lifestyles and our careers. We've become a force to be reckoned with politically. But we still remain the prisoners of the Covenant, limited by the belief that we can find happiness only if we look good.

Because we're individuals, finding fulfillment and meaning is inherently personal and must be inwardly directed. It must emanate from our inner core. This search for meaning must harmonize with our own individual dharma—who we are by nature, what our particular circumstances are, and the context of how we fit into this world.

what is your personal purpose?

Finding your own dharma or personal purpose is a lifelong endeavor. Your dharma is the driving force that inspires the appetite of your mind and the passion of your soul. From an Eastern perspective, dharma is also your individual role in the cosmos. Each of us has an important individual contribution to make toward maintaining the order of the universe. Finding our individual sense of meaning is therefore a very great personal responsibility indeed.

Trying to identify your personal purpose may be difficult at first. You may find it easier to recognize the *feeling* you get than to describe it in words.

But once you've worked with your personal purpose for a while, you'll start to notice when you're acting in synch with it, and when you're not. When you act in accordance with your dharma, you feel aligned with your personal sense of truth. It's as if your personal purpose is a pole star and a huge inner magnet draws you with great force in that direction. Of course, everything won't necessarily go the way you want it to even when you're aligned with your personal purpose. But deep down, you'll know that things are as they should be.

Pursuing your personal purpose can help you change your relationship to food and your body as no externally driven diet can.

When you find the true satisfaction that comes from fulfilling your personal purpose, you won't need to seek contentment in food or how you look.

PRACTICE: FINDING YOUR PERSONAL PURPOSE

part one—defining what's meaningful

You can begin to outline what you consider to be your personal purpose by answering the following questions. Your answers to these questions will help you formulate a statement of personal purpose. This statement will reflect your inner nature in the context of relationships and events in your life and the world as a whole.

Repeat this practice over time, allowing your personal purpose to evolve and deepen. The practice is divided into three parts. You may want to do each part separately to give yourself enough time with each section.

Begin by answering the following questions:

1. What gifts and strengths do I bring to the world?
2. How are my gifts and strengths reflected in what I do in the world?
3. What things do people tell me I am good at or that they like about me?
4. What are the three activities I most love to do?

5. What things do I feel passionately drawn to do in life?

6. Do I often do the things I feel passionately drawn to, or do I only dream of doing them "someday"?

7. Are there activities that I used to do as a child, or beliefs or concepts that I was drawn to when I was younger, that I don't include in my life today?

8. When I do the activities I'm passionately drawn to, and those I loved to do as a child, how do I feel inside; what internal gratification do I get?

These first eight questions give you insight into your nature as you experience it from within and as you manifest it in the world. Your answers reflect your unique nature—what makes you feel passionate and gives your life meaning.

Most of us are aware of some of the things we're good at and enjoy doing. But we may be unable to appreciate or be aware of many of our other individual gifts and talents. We may take our abilities for granted or simply take no notice at all.

To summarize your answers to the above questions, first list your three greatest abilities. In summarizing, also consider what others tell you are your talents. These aptitudes and predilections are a reflection of your true nature—who you really are.

Now answer the remaining questions:

9. What were one or more instances in my life when I felt a sense of connection to my true nature?

10. If I could do three things to help make the world a better place to live in, what would they be?

11. Today, am I consciously doing my work and relating to people in a way that feels aligned with who I am and my inner sense of truth?

12. If I died today, would I feel that I had done what I wanted to do with my life? Would I feel that I'd fulfilled my purpose?

Your answers to these final questions give you insight into how your inner nature is reflected in the world. They also show you how to go about creating a life that supports who you really are and fulfills your personal purpose.

Now you're ready to make an initial statement of your personal purpose. This will change and expand over time.

Your personal purpose is your impassioned vision of what's most important to you in life, what you'd like to dedicate your life to. This statement should be inspired by the strong feeling you get when you're connected to your true nature. Anything goes—this is your chance to access your dreams. A personal-purpose statement need not seem immediately attainable. It's meant to be a long-term goal that can take you through life, providing you with sustaining vision and motivation.

Your answers to questions 8, 9, and 12 will be particularly helpful to review in formulating your personal-purpose statement.

Write your personal-purpose statement at the top of a blank page in your journal.

Reflection: When you spend a lot of time obsessing about food and your body, you can lose sight of what holds real meaning. But when you clearly state your personal purpose, it will help you focus on what holds meaning for you.

Your personal-purpose statement provides a reminder of what you care about most in life. When life presents its inevitable challenges that cause you to doubt what you're doing, your personal purpose can let you know if you're on track or not. Recalling your personal purpose helps you to shift your perspective so you see that your diet and what your body looks like aren't the most important things in the world.

part two—defining your circumstances

Now, to put your personal purpose into the context of your life as it is today, you'll examine the particular circumstances that make up *your* life.

1. Take a moment to clear your mind, then close your eyes and let your thoughts wander over the components of the context in which you live your life:

· Family
· Relationships outside of family
· Work
· Society

These are your life circumstances. Now write a statement describing what about your circumstances make you feel satisfied or happy. Also consider which keep you feeling stuck, dissatisfied, or unhappy.

2. Next, summarize your personal circumstances pertaining to food and body. Close your eyes again, and this time, focus your attention on your own food and body conflict.

· How do your thoughts and behavior with regard to food and your body keep you stuck?
· How do you wish your relationship to food and your body were different?

Reflection: The circumstances of your life and your food and body conflict are where you start from. This is your reality right now. As you pursue your personal purpose, your reality must be taken into account. You need to fulfill your dreams and make changes from where you are, not from where you are not.

When you start from the present and work toward change, your surrounding circumstances will also evolve. As this happens, your definition of your problem and intention will inevitably shift. To reflect this evolution, frequently revisit your original problem and intention as you defined them in Chapter One.

Take a moment right now to consider your life circumstances, the circumstances of your relationship to food and your body, and your statement of purpose. With all of these in mind, restate your problem and intention, and write them in your journal.

welcome home

By putting into words your own personal purpose, you've brought yourself home. You are here, right now, with the unbearable parts of your life that you'd give almost anything to change. And just as definitively, you're the impassioned dreamer of your life's greatest potential.

But how do you maintain the connection to your dreams while remaining in touch with your present circumstances? Not in theory, on a page in your journal, but as you move through the twists and turns of your everyday life?

This is the challenge that Eastern mind/body practices address. They teach you to go deeply inside so you can stay connected to your dharma while remaining grounded in your present circumstances.

FOUR

the importance of a practice

Awake! Awake! O sleeper of the Land of Shadows, wake! expand!

—WILLIAM BLAKE, "JERUSALEM"

the morning after

Any of us who have ever embarked on *the* diet to end all diets knows the thrill of excitement from standing on the brink of change. Nothing feels so good as to finally take your life back into your own hands, breaking free of the trap that's held you for so long. You may have some trepidations about the difficulties that lie ahead. But when you're ready and willing to make a change, you can almost breathe the air of freedom that lies around the corner as you head into the promised land.

The precise moment when we're highly motivated to make a deep change in our lives represents a great opportunity. For once we aren't living in the past or dreaming of the future. We're present right now, with all our energies focused. We've gathered all of our inner resources to meet the challenge, and we're ready to throw ourselves into the effort with everything we've got. We *really* want to change.

But if you're a diet veteran, you don't need anyone to remind you of the cold hard truth—sadly, most diets don't prove to be the end to all diets. If they worked, then you'd never need to go on another. When the diet fails once again, our enormous excitement and will to change shift to disappointment and hopelessness. We blame ourselves over and over again for the failure: "I didn't have enough willpower, I didn't exercise as much as I should have, I'm just meant to be fat."

What went wrong? Was it the diet, was it you, or was it both? Just when you think you've got all the variables under control—finding the perfect ratio between limiting your food and exercising your body—something falls apart. You find yourself back in the same painful place of self-doubt and regret, hoping to try again tomorrow. It's a vicious cycle, and you're at the center of it, feeling more and more despair with every turn of the wheel.

We call this pattern of helpless repetition the *morning-after syndrome,* and it's all too familiar to most women. Last night, at some point, you went wildly out of control. You lost consciousness, spaced out, and abandoned your diet. After your shame and disgust fade, after the feeling of being bloated and stuffed to the gills slowly subsides, you find yourself back at square one—again.

To break this cycle for good, we take the methodologies of traditional Eastern mind/body practices and apply them to conscious strategies for resolving food and body conflicts.

the practice of purpose

For as along as she could remember, Roberta had always been obese. It was the motivation of pursuing her personal purpose that gave Roberta, for the first time in her life, the perspective she needed to break free of her food and body conflict.

As a child, Roberta spent much of her time alone reading, and when she did play with other children, she was often ridiculed or ostracized because of her weight. From time to time she'd halfheartedly try a weight-loss diet. But she was firmly convinced that, like her mother, she was big-boned, with a slow metabolism, and was just meant to be "fat."

On bad days, Roberta would hook into the messages of the Covenant and become extremely depressed. She knew there was no way she could ever come near matching the ideals she saw paraded before her in magazines and on TV. She'd often react by retreating to her room to find solace in special snacks. Her main comfort in life besides food was reading. While reading, she always felt happy, impassioned, and alive. Hidden in her room with her books, she finally felt free within her imagination and her love of language.

When Roberta first went in for counseling, she felt very ambivalent about her ability to make any changes in her life. But she was intrigued by the concept of looking at her weight problem as the symptom of a deeper, underlying hunger for meaning. When she allowed her imagination to run wild and explore the possibilities for defining a personal purpose, Roberta felt an enthusiasm and drive she'd rarely experienced.

She realized that there was something she'd always wanted to do with her life but had been too scared to make happen: she desperately wanted to teach children how to derive the same pleasure from reading that she'd always experienced. This love of reading had supported her through tough times and loneliness in her life.

Roberta worked as a clerk in a drugstore. She found the work boring, but she felt safe in the quiet environment. As she contemplated how in the world she could go out and become a teacher, she had a flash of insight into what her choices were: she could either continue to retreat from the world and hide her true talents, or she could allow her dream to carry her out of self-imposed isolation and suffering.

She saw seemingly infinite pieces of her personal puzzle that she knew she couldn't change overnight, such as her obesity, her feelings of inferiority, and her depression. Yet her desire to teach was incredibly strong, coming from her core. She recognized that merely acknowledging her personal purpose had already given her a deep sense of immediate change and gratification.

Knowing she had to start where she was to make her dream a reality, Roberta saw that she had many steps between now and becoming a teacher. In her mind, the challenge was huge—finding the money and time to get a teaching certificate, then finding a teaching job and getting hired. But Roberta realized that pursuing her vision, and feeling impassioned, was worth the effort. She made up her mind that she'd just work step by step to overcome each hurdle. She vowed to keep her personal purpose before her through all the hard work ahead.

Although her attention was focused purely on her goal of becoming a teacher, Roberta also found her relationship to food starting to change. She noticed that she was so filled with the excitement of her newly awakened passion that mealtime was no longer the highlight of her day. She hadn't been feeling the need to console herself with food rewards, since her time and energy were fully engaged in pursuing her goals.

And when she did find herself slipping into her old behaviors—retreating to her room with a plate of food when the going got rough—she felt able to bring her mind back to her personal purpose. Compared to what she now saw as meaningful, she questioned how fulfilling it would be to run away, overeat, or become depressed over a minor incident.

Eventually, in this intuitive manner, Roberta was able to bring her personal purpose to mind every time she sat down to eat or began to launch into a destructive habit of self-loathing. As she began to trust that her purpose was real, doable, and vital to her, the old habits of food and thought lost the power they had once held. Roberta didn't change overnight; nor did she become a supermodel. But she did lose weight and gain a lot of self-respect by pursuing meaning and bringing perspective into her life.

waking up right now

The practices that follow are designed to help you work with your personal purpose to set out on a new path and leave your old traps behind. They're structured to teach you new skills that have nothing to do with counting calories, measuring and weighing, or calculating calories burned per hour of activity. Instead, you'll learn how to stay *conscious* within your daily activities. In particular, you'll learn how to stay connected with how you relate to food and your body, so you can know what your body needs at any given moment.

When our lives are dominated by ghosts of the past and fantasies of the future, it's as if we're asleep within our present existence. We've been looking behind or before for so long that we're blind to our present condition. Using the practices, you can learn how to wake up in your life as it is right now, and start taking action to reclaim the present moment.

the diet part

"Finally," you think, "they must finally be getting to the *diet* part. What's their new formula?" As you thumb through page after page of this new kind of "diet" program, you may be looking for what makes this one so different. Is it less painful? Quicker? Is there some exotic fruit that actually burns calories and tastes great (available exclusively through an 800 number)? Is it that fabulous space suit with a vacuum-cleaner attachment that just suctions away all those

unwanted pounds? Or ("please, please, please") is there some kind of new supplement that fixes it all at night while you sleep?

We'd all love a quick and painless fix, but unfortunately that's not in this book. Ancient alchemists used to look for a way to turn base metals into gold. Modern alchemists are longing to find the magic bullet—the pill, powder, or mysterious synthesized wonder food—that will turn fat into lean muscle.

We don't offer any effortless solutions. We believe that the reason scientists haven't yet come up with the magic formula for slenderness is because they're trying to solve the external manifestation of a deeper internal problem. The classic Western solution to weight problems seems a simple enough formula: reduce or increase calories in, increase or decrease calories burned, and voilà! A perfectly shaped woman every time.

But we're not machines, we're human beings. What the Western perspective neglects to take into account is our free will, stemming from our soul with all of its messy, illogical, ethereal needs. We ignore and block out deeper spiritual longings at a great cost to ourselves. The problem isn't our bodies or what we're eating, but lives that are lacking in meaning and fulfillment.

For women, this battleground for our souls seems to get turned back around again and again to food and our bodies. Why? A well-known television commercial from the 1970s for Enjoli perfume provides insight into this question: "She can bring home the bacon, fry it up in the pan, and never ever let you forget you're a man." This ditty says it all: to be considered a success as women, we're expected to have accomplished careers and find time to maintain our looks and sex appeal while assuming our traditional role as the nurturers who cook and dish out meals. No matter how far we've come, we can't seem to escape our dual roles as the babe and the cook. It's no wonder that, for so many of us, food and our bodies become the objects of a troubled self-expression.

And we can't escape by just turning around and going to the opposite extreme: "I won't ever think about my appearance again, I don't care what I look like or what I eat, and that ungrateful family of mine can just start cooking for themselves!" By jumping to the opposite extreme, you can be certain you'll just be trading one set of problems for another.

Whether we like it or not, we do live in *this* world, not some ethereal world where nothing but our soul counts. A solution that truly works has to take into account both our internal spiritual needs and the needs of women who live in our world, in our society, and at this time in history. It's only natural to swing from one extreme to the other, but our ultimate goal is to find balance in all things. The Buddhists call this effort "walking the middle path."

The following practices will teach you to restore balance to all aspects of your life, placing food and body issues back in their proper perspective.

the practice

Eastern mind/body practices were originally developed to increase conscious awareness of the present moment. In our culture we refer to the most overt levels of conscious and unconscious states as being awake or asleep. But there's a more subtle level on which we can learn to understand what it means to be conscious: that is, not only being awake, but being aware of everything as it happens in the present moment. This is the Eastern perspective of consciousness.

Being conscious in the present moment is not just an awareness of what's happening but a capacity to simply observe it. When we're conscious, we can allow ourselves to simply watch the thoughts, sensations, and events of the moment as they unfold.

Staying conscious in this way is difficult under any circumstances. It's especially challenging when you're observing habits and patterns that you'd rather not see—like your most despicable or deeply buried food habits. But consciousness is essential if we're to free ourselves from the well-worn ruts that keep us stuck.

For example, the most insidious phase of the morning-after

syndrome is that at some point in the cycle you become unconscious. You pig out, go for it, give in, or in some way "blow it." Whatever rules or imagined parameters you've set for yourself fall by the wayside as you tumble into an unconscious state of eating and let it rip. This is the "food coma," in which an entire cake has disappeared and you have crumbs on your lips, frosting smeared on the tip of your nose, and an aching belly, but not a single memory of chewing or how the food tasted. While the food somehow clearly got eaten, you simply blacked out and went unconscious, waking up only after the deed was done.

Consciousness is the antidote for the food coma—you can't black out and remain conscious at the same time. Even if we don't change immediately, and continue to engage in behaviors that we find distressing, we can immediately start on the path to change by simply observing our actions.

We'll begin our practices with honing this skill of staying conscious. We'll start out by slowing everything down, so we can learn how to quiet our minds and bring consciousness to our bodies in action.

PRACTICE: SIMPLE WALKING MEDITATION PRACTICE

You may think consciousness is easy enough if you decide to make your mind up to it. But it's actually extremely difficult, because we're so much in the habit of remaining unconscious. Learning how to stay conscious is a skill that must be cultivated like any other, and that's why we've called these exercises "practices."

This walking exercise is a traditional practice taught in a form of Buddhist meditation called Vipassana, or insight meditation. Vipassana means seeing things clearly. The goal is to stay as focused and alert as possible while you simply walk.

You may do this practice indoors or outdoors, barefoot or with shoes on. Choose a location where you'll be undisturbed so you can give the effort your complete focus.

1. Start by standing with your feet together and your arms hanging by your side. With your eyes closed, pay attention to your breath rising and falling. Simply notice any sensations, emotions, or thoughts that may arise. Once you feel focused, open your eyes.

2. Start by very slowly lifting your foot, moving it forward, and setting it down. Try to notice every aspect of this motion—what muscles you move, what subtle shifts in your body take place, what other parts of your body have to move in order to maintain your balance as you lift your foot and put it down again.

3. Next, lift the opposite foot, moving it slowly forward and setting it down, remaining conscious throughout the process.

4. Continue to walk, moving one foot in front of another in this way, for about six feet.

5. When you've walked that far, remain conscious as you slowly turn around, then walk back using the same slow, focused method.

6. The main goal through this practice is to stay as focused as you can on the actual physical process of walking. Notice when your mind races off on other thoughts, when feelings arise (irritation, restlessness, or pleasure), or when sensations grab your attention ("My foot hurts" or "It feels good to be moving").

Reflection: What you'll probably find is that though you're walking a short distance, your mind will have been elsewhere for much of the practice even if you're very determined to stay conscious and focused. That's perfectly normal: neither good nor bad, simply a demonstration of the nature of our minds. We spend much of our lives daydreaming and thinking of anything else but what we're actually doing at any given moment.

Return to this walking meditation practice each day for two weeks, and notice if your ability to focus improves with repeated effort.

the composition of a practice

Traditional mind/body practices are frameworks for acting with consciousness. They're designed to reveal whatever it is that makes up *your* present moment. Practices act as a kind of internal mirror. This reflection magnifies your thoughts, sensations, and emotions so that you can see them more clearly.

Through the practices, you can begin to strengthen your ability to remain conscious. As you bring conscious awareness to deeper and deeper levels of your thoughts and actions, there will be less and less difference between this inner reflection and what you see in the mirror. You'll learn to actually *be* in the present moment with all the subtleties of mind, body, and emotion that flood your awareness.

practice building blocks

The building blocks that make a practice work are *structure, intention,* and *attention.* The structure is the framework for the practice. It lends the practice consistency and form, providing a steady blueprint amid the constant changes of your life. For example, in the walking meditation, the structure is to walk for six feet with awareness.

We originally used the term "intention" to describe your intention for change. Now we'll take the same concept and apply it to the practices. Before you begin each practice, you'll first set a clearly defined intention—a reason for performing the practice that goes beyond the simple act of completing the action. As you practice, you'll continually bring your mind back to your intention for practice—the reason you're doing it. In the walking practice, for example, your intention is to remain conscious.

It can be helpful to bring your personal purpose to mind as you set your intention for a practice. It's an important acknowledgment that the practice you're doing right now is part of the bigger picture of your whole life.

The final building block is your conscious attention. Your attention makes the whole thing work. In the example of the walking meditation, without your attention, you might be just strolling down the street. But your attention within the structure of the activity allows you to constantly bring your focus back to observing the act of walking. This attention to your actions makes a practice a true catalyst for change.

These three elements together provide a checklist to follow before and during any kind of practice: (1) define structure, (2) set intention, (3) bring attention to your actions.

practice makes perfect

Traditional mind/body practices set up an arena for growth and change by presenting an unchanging structure. Within that designated safe space, all aspects of ourselves can surface, be observed, and then dissipate. In this way, the mere act of bringing our attention to our thoughts, feelings, and sensations becomes a catalyst for healing and change.

The practices are intended to be performed repeatedly over time. You do your practice on good days and bad days, when you feel like doing it and when you don't. Learning to stick with the practice, no matter what your state of mind, is paramount. It's easy to do a mind/body practice when you feel good, strong, and centered. But on days that are filled with stress, when you've got low energy, your emotions are running high, or your body isn't feeling well tuned, it may be tempting to avoid practice altogether. What you'll find is that merely doing the practice with regularity brings continuity, calm, and insight to your life. You'll practice not because you're supposed to, but because it's the still point in your life around which the rest of the chaos swirls. Consistent practice helps you to steadily face the inconsistencies that make up all of our lives in an ever changing world.

Through the practices, we become familiar with our individual patterns of perception, thought, and behavior. With repeated effort, we can come to realize that these are just patterns rather than permanent, unchangeable parts of ourselves. With practice we can learn to wake up within our own lives, be who we already are, and know ourselves for the first time. Maintaining consciousness provides a direct connection to our personal sense of spirituality.

FIVE

the feedback loop

You must train your intuition—you must trust the small voice inside you which tells you exactly what to say, what to decide.

—INGRID BERGMAN, ACTRESS

learning to listen

What are you hungry for? What's at the bottom of your constant craving, and what does your soul long for? What brought you to pick up this book, and what's going to finally satisfy your burning hunger deep within?

There's a voice in you right now that already has all of the answers. From relatively insignificant choices like what to eat for lunch, to life-altering decisions like whether you should quit your job, there's a voice deep inside you that knows exactly the right course of action to take at every juncture—if only you could hear it.

Fortunately, you also have a tool to detect and decipher the messages that you're receiving from your internal system: *feedback*. Typically we speak of positive or negative feedback, such as compliments or criticism. But there's much more to feedback than we're usually aware of.

The concept of feedback is used in medicine and science, emphasizing the idea of a loop, with input and output, cause and effect. Feedback is also used in electronics to describe electrical circuits, implying a loop of input flowing through a system, then reentering as new input.

We each have our own personal feedback loop operating internally. It's the means by which we filter and interpret our experience in the world, helping us make decisions and direct our actions.

the feedback loop

Have you ever left the TV on for hours, just running in the background, with nobody watching? As you go about your day, cleaning the house, cooking dinner, talking with your family, the sounds continue to broadcast. Across the screen flicker soap operas, game shows, news bulletins, comedies, all talking away, but nobody's listening. Occasionally you might make the conscious decision to tune in, if you see a show that piques your interest, or if you catch a bit of floating dialogue that captures your attention. But whether or not you're watching, the TV plays on, sometimes nonsensical programming, sometimes important information.

Your feedback loop operates in much the same way. It's the stream of data, association, memories, feelings, sensations, and judgments that runs through you constantly, broadcasting seven days a week, twenty-four hours a day. Whether or not you're paying attention, your internal broadcast system is talking to you all the time. Just as you might with an ever broadcasting TV, sometimes you tune into your feedback. At other times the messages whir by so fast, or at such a deep level, that you don't consciously recognize them. But at some level you *are* processing all the information from your feedback stream and making choices based upon it, whether you're conscious of it or not.

For example, you see a sumptuous piece of pizza just dripping with cheese. Without even thinking about it, your mouth starts to water and you suddenly find yourself ravenously hungry. Next you may think, "Oh, I'd just die for a piece of pizza!" Then, just as quickly, the next thought enters your mind: "I can't touch that piece of pizza, it will make me fat instantly. I must resist the temptation!"

An entire interior monologue of this sort can race through you in a split instant. You may be only remotely aware of it as you carry on with your business at hand. But whether or not you're conscious of anything taking place in your feedback loop, you'll make a choice about eating the pizza based on this internal process.

That's why it's so vital to be able to get in on this process and intervene in the loop. If you're conscious of the feedback, between the time you get the input and the time you act on it, you'll have a lot more say over all the decisions you ultimately make.

The feedback loop provides an easy and quick way of being ourselves within our complex world. It allows us to filter all of the information we're bombarded with, and proceed actively in our lives. If we were to get swept away by the minutiae, we'd be unable to act. But our internal feedback loop is able to go through a complex decision-making process in a split second.

Sometimes that speed doesn't serve us so well. We get an impulse, and we react unconsciously out of deeply ingrained habits. For example, you get anxious waiting to hear from last week's hot date, and you mindlessly shove M&M's into your mouth. Or you get passed over for a promotion at work, and you instantly decide it's because you're too fat.

In behavioral psychology, this type of pattern is called a conditioned response. Like Pavlov's dogs, conditioned to drool at the sound of a bell, we are kept unconscious of our feedback system by our habitual responses.

Our conditional behaviors and perceptions are perpetuated from within but are also constantly fueled by external messages from our culture. These messages are the Covenant in action. We're bombarded by "ought-tos": how we ought to eat, how we ought to look, how we ought to feel.

The moment we buy into the Covenant, we must override our own feedback system. We accept the underlying premises that women *should* be thin, that we *are* too fat, that dieting *is* the answer, that fattening foods *are* dangerous, or that we *must* have willpower to overcome our body's hunger pangs. Instead of letting our internal sensibilities shape our beliefs, we try to conform our internal sensibilities to the Covenant.

When we act habitually, unable to use our feedback as a guide, we find ourselves heading down well-worn paths that lead us back to familiar dead-end destinations.

PRACTICE: FEEDBACK OVER TIME

This practice helps you to bring your awareness and attention into the present moment as you go about your day. It familiarizes you with your own feedback, how it affects your thoughts and directs your actions.

The day you do this practice, carry an alarm clock or timer (a wristwatch with an alarm function is ideal) and your journal with you throughout the day.

1. Before you begin, set your intention to be honest with yourself and to observe your judgments or conclusions as objectively as possible.

2. Right after you get up in the morning, set the alarm to go off two hours later. Then simply go about your day as planned.

3. When the alarm sounds, bring your focus to the present moment. If possible, stop what you're doing. Close your eyes and take a quick inventory of the feedback information that presents itself in that instant. Then answer the following questions. It's best if you can record your answers in your journal. But if that's not possible, simply take a moment to reflect on the answers.

· What is my general emotional state? Am I calm, tense, stressed, depressed, happy, excited? Choose one or two words that best fit your overall emotional state of being at the moment the alarm rang.

· What is my general physical state? Am I tired, rested, sore, relaxed? List any physical sensations that dominate your awareness.

· What is my general mental state? Am I bored, engaged, distracted, fatigued? List any mental states that dominate your
awareness.

4. Reset your timer or alarm for two hours from the time you
finish answering the questions, then carry on with your day.
At least four times during the course of the day, continue to
repeat the practice when the alarm sounds.

Reflection: When you have time, look over the list of feedback
responses that you noted during the day. How much of it was familiar, and how much of it was information that you weren't previously
aware of? For instance, were you well aware of the fact that you
were hungry at mealtime? Or, if you found yourself experiencing
feelings of anger during the day, were you conscious of them?

This practice can teach you how important it is to regularly
take time to tune into your feedback. At any given moment, you
have an opportunity to go from an unconscious state into mindful
awareness. With the valuable information our feedback provides,
we can make choices that are in line with our whole being.

the gut feeling

A deeper aspect of the feedback stream that runs through you is what's commonly referred to as your gut feeling. The gut feeling, also known as the sixth sense, is the voice of your soul. It's the intuitive sense that alerts you to your deepest sense of right and wrong. Your gut feeling can tell you if you're on track or not. When you learn to listen to it, you'll begin to recognize it as an excellent barometer of what's going on inside of you.

Though gut feelings can serve as clear and accurate guides, we often ignore them. You may know in your gut something's wrong, but you disregard its warning and go against your instincts. Afterward, things go miserably awry. It's not until later that you recall your bad feeling and how you ignored it.

That's how the young bride-to-be felt when she dropped her wedding invitations into the mailbox, then instantly wished she could climb inside and retrieve them. The moment they went through the slot, she had a sickening, sinking feeling in her gut. Ignoring this powerful sensation, a huge sense of "no" deep within, she went ahead with the marriage as planned. Five years later she finally followed through on her initial instinct and got a divorce.

what are you hungry for?

As women, we often seem to have a more natural predilection toward listening to our gut feeling or intuition than men do, but we're still frequently guilty of overriding it. We plow through with an action that our inner self screams at us not to take. As in the case of the bride, everything and everyone else in your life may be telling you the "right" thing to do, though that lone voice deep inside haunts you with a nagging sense of doubt.

The practices will help you to tap into your gut feelings. As you learn to listen to all of your inner feelings and sensations, you'll discover how to trust your gut feelings as you would a compass for knowing when you're on the right track.

follow the feedback clues

Learning to recognize and trust her gut feelings was the key for Ann in resolving her food and body conflict. She'd been plagued for years by twenty pounds that she couldn't seem to keep off. Ann had tried every diet, weight-loss gadget, and pill she could find. But nothing had worked over the long run. For once and for all, she wanted to lose those "unacceptable" pounds.

Ann began her dieting career at the ripe old age of fifteen. She'd returned home from summer camp having gained eighteen pounds. Her mother had immediately enrolled her in a weight-loss clinic, where she was initiated into the ranks of women warriors who spend years subsisting on delicacies such as apple and raw potato, grapefruit and eggs, or dry toast and salad with dressing on the side.

Ann knew by heart the calorie count and portion size of virtually any food she might encounter. She could calculate precisely how long to stay on the exercise bike to burn off the extra calories that inevitably sneaked through the gates of her mouth.

By the time she was thirty-two, Ann felt she was ready for a major change. She was exhausted by the unending game of what she could or couldn't eat. Exasperated by the relentless battle with her weight, she was ready to try anything.

She started by noticing that she had deeply ingrained concepts about which foods were good and bad. Because of these preconceptions, she found it difficult to actually hear her feedback. But by continuing to make the effort, she started accessing her genuine feedback and trusting her intuition to tell her what was good and bad for *her.*

Ann decided she would eat what she really felt like eating, when her feedback indicated that she was genuinely hungry. For the first time since Ann was a young girl, she slowly felt her appetite coming into balance. By eating in this intuitive manner, she gradually lost ten pounds.

Although she was happy to lose the weight, Ann clung to the

belief that she still had another ten pounds to go. Years earlier, she'd seen a chart that showed the ideal weight for her frame and height as ten pounds below her current weight.

But as she continued to tune into her feedback, she realized she was actually feeling very comfortable and healthy at her current weight. How could this be? How could she be happy when she hadn't reached the ideal number on the chart? She'd always tied her sense of self-worth and success to that magic number.

Eventually, she had to concede that the number had lost its meaning for her. She realized that pursuing the number on the chart, counting the calories, or exercising to lose weight had never brought her any lasting happiness. The simple acts of listening to her internal needs and responding to her feedback helped her shift perspective. She now found herself open to exploring how much she wanted to weigh, what she wanted to eat, and what truly held meaning for her in life.

flying in the dark

When you're learning to guide your life by listening to your gut feelings, how can you be certain you're doing the right thing? For those who follow the dictates of the Covenant or our society, there are clear indicators of progress or failure. You have tangible badges of success: the "right" body, the "right" job that lets you buy the "right" car so you can live in the "right" neighborhood with the "right" house. But when you follow the path directed by your own feedback, what are the signs that you're on the real right course?

When you start following your internal direction, you may be concerned that others will judge your choices and think you're way off-course. Perhaps your plate contains foods that aren't in line with the current cure-all diet, or your concern for the very latest fashions has slid miserably downhill, or your high-profile career has slipped into oblivion. Not only do you not fit into those size 2 jeans, but you may feel like you don't fit in at all, and this can be scary. What could you have been thinking, to follow your own path and pursue meaning and personal purpose? Have you gone crazy? Now that you've shifted your idea of success to learning how to truly be yourself, you may start doubting the worthiness of that goal. After all, when everyone else is still following the Covenant and you're not, the ramifications can be severe. Covenants are maintained by everyone agreeing implicitly that certain behaviors and standards are approved of and others aren't. Following your own internal dictates can be a lonely and uncertain road to walk.

When you have doubts about the worthiness of your path, stop and reflect on what you really want. By listening to your internal feedback, in particular your gut feeling, you can distinguish what's right for you.

You can't ever *know* with 100 percent certainty that what you're doing is the right thing. There are no objective standards to provide that kind of certainty. But you can *trust* the voice inside of you, your gut instinct, that tells you whether or not you're on the right course. Flying in the dark, following your own path, means learning to have faith in your own internal wisdom.

SIX

finding a food practice that works

So high you can't go over it, so low you can't go under it, so wide you can't go around it, let's go through the door.

—TRADITIONAL FOLK SONG

what is a food practice?

A *food practice* helps us to establish a new relationship with eating. It is not a diet. There are no right or wrong foods, no weighing and measuring, no weekly encounters with the scale.

Food practices are structured activities that teach us how to be fully conscious, and full of intention, while we eat. Like mind/body practices, the food practices in this book are based on the traditional Eastern approach.

Through the food practices, you'll learn to go deep inside and encounter the patterns and habits that are at the root of your food and body conflict. You'll discover how to use feedback to bring awareness to your unconscious behaviors and make changes from the inside out.

recipe for meaning

Before you begin these practices, it's critical to identify your reasons for doing them: your intention for the practice. You may be starting a food practice with the same intention you've had for starting diets your whole life: to lose weight and look good. Or you may be seeking relief from the pain caused by your food and body conflict. Be honest with yourself about what your true intention is—that's how to "start where you are."

As you continue with the practices, your intention may evolve. Try to observe without judgment how it changes (and it may evolve from day to day, hour to hour). It's important to stay attuned to whatever is motivating you and notice how it aligns with your sense of personal purpose.

Before you start the first food practice, ask yourself a simple question to get some initial perspective on your priorities and values: "Is the most important thing in life what I look like and what I eat?" As you work toward defining what gives *your* life meaning, continue to reconsider this fundamental question.

raising the stakes

Sandra sought counseling because she ate in an erratic and compulsive way. She was a serious mountain climber and outdoor-survival instructor and was extremely physically fit.

Sandra had a solid understanding of basic nutrition. She integrated into her teaching a study of everyday nutrition, underlining the importance of eating a balanced diet. But when it came to her own life, she simply couldn't apply the commonsense rules of healthy eating that she taught in her classes.

During rigorous hours of work, Sandra would skip lunch breaks so she could leave early enough to get in an afternoon climb. She'd then find herself in her car, mindlessly stuffing handfuls of dried fruit and nuts into her mouth, or eating several high-performance energy bars on the way to her workout.

After her climb, she would return home too exhausted to cook. Still ravenous, she would wind up staving off her appetite with most of a bag of tortilla chips, salsa, cheese, and a beer while she tidied up and unwound from her day. Occasionally she would join friends for a true meal, but most of her food intake was in the form of snacks on the run.

Sandra's style of eating epitomizes what we call an unconscious approach to food. She seldom, if ever, focused carefully on what or how she ate, and frequently didn't even taste her food. Sandra was aware that her approach to food and eating was imbalanced—she never would have recommended that her students eat as she did to support an active lifestyle. But she just couldn't seem to find the time to make healthy eating a priority.

She went in for dietary counseling after snapping out of her routine one evening with the startling recognition—three quarters of the way through her chips-and-cheese "dinner"—that the cheese she'd been scarfing down was moldy and rotten-tasting. She was shocked and ashamed, and felt hypocritical. How could she present lectures on good nutrition and then go home to what she called her nightly "eating frenzies"?

Sandra's realization was painful, but it jolted her out of her well-established habits long enough to allow her to take a new look at her life. She was forced to examine what was at stake if she continued blindly on the path she'd established. She knew her health was at risk, that she couldn't go on eating such a limited range of foods forever, and that she'd managed to stay relatively healthy only because she was young and had a strong constitution.

Although Sandra believed her love of the outdoors was what she valued most in life, she saw that she was acting unconsciously here as well. She came to see that she'd been treating nature as something she wanted to conquer—to climb as many high peaks as she could and teach others how to master the environment.

These realizations caused Sandra to consider what was at stake for her, and why it was so important for her to want to make changes in her life. She saw that her lack of mindfulness was detrimental to her health and prevented her from finding fulfillment in life. Sandra understood that it was essential to become more conscious: not only about what she was eating, but also about what she truly cared for in life—her sense of purpose.

As we begin this first practice, the question is, what stakes are on the line for you personally? What does transforming your relationship with food ultimately matter to you?

notes on practicing

Before you start a practice, remind yourself of the practice checklist described in Chapter Four, page 63. Remember to bring to mind your intention for the specific practice at hand. Also remember to bring your active and conscious attention to the practice.

These two elements—intention and attention—are what power the practices and make them a potent vehicle for change.

PRACTICE: WHAT ARE THE STAKES?

Repeat this practice whenever you feel your commitment to change drifting. It will enable you to reconnect to the present moment and help you assess what you truly want in your life. In answering the following questions, be as specific as possible.

1. In your journal, write out the main food problem that you identified in the first chapter, or any new problem with food you're currently experiencing.
2. Consider what will happen if you continue to repeat this behavior indefinitely. Ask yourself the following questions:

   · If my problem continues over time, what impact will it have on my happiness?
   · At the end of my life, if I look back and consider endless years of struggle with this problem, how will it have obstructed my ability to fulfill my potential and personal purpose?

Reflection: Identifying what's on the line for you personally can serve as a powerful motivation. The stakes are much greater than fitting into a dress or looking good in a reflection. It's your life's work and potential that's on the line. Most of us would agree that living a meaningful life is far more important than putting all of our energy and focus in to the relentless cycle of a food and body conflict.

gather the data

Now it's time for you to place your food and body conflict into the bigger picture of your life. You'll begin by keeping a written record of your food and body patterns. You'll gather data on precisely what, when, and how you eat. You'll look at how foods and eating habits may trigger your patterns of thought, emotion, and physical sensation. And you'll learn how to listen to your feedback in action.

Approach these practices as you would an experiment. You'll serve as both the scientist and the subject, recording your own external and internal data. Remember, these eating records are for your eyes only. You won't be showing them to anyone else, so there's no one to impress or disappoint. You won't shock anyone with your "appalling" behaviors, and you won't win approval for "incredible" willpower. This is a completely safe opportunity to be who you really are. If you can see what your relationship to food and your body *really* is, then you'll finally have the information that you need to change.

Note: The following two practices should be carried out during the same time period. Make a copy of the Food and Body Feedback Graph (see page 88) and enough copies of the Eating Record Chart (see page 87) to last you a week.

PRACTICE: EATING RECORD CHART

Keep a diary of everything you eat for a week. During this time, try to eat just as you normally do. It's more important to note the types of foods you eat rather than the quantity. You'll also record other information about your eating experience, such as with whom and where you're eating. Note anything that occurs repeatedly or seems relevant to your own personal eating experience.

PRACTICE: FOOD AND BODY FEEDBACK GRAPH

In conjunction with your Eating Record Chart, fill in the Food and Body Feedback Graph. This graph will serve as a companion for the data you collect in your Eating Record Chart.

eating record

DATE:

MENU	BREAKFAST	LUNCH	DINNER	SNACK
ACTIVITY Before				
During				
LOCATION				
COMPANY Alone/Others				
HUNGER Before				
During				
FEELINGS Physical Before/After				
Emotional Before/After				

food and body feedback

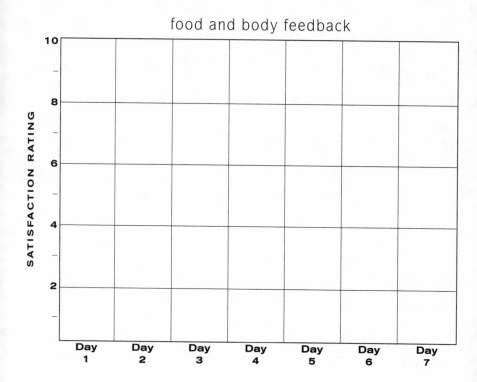

1. Each day, take a moment to fill out your Food and Body Feedback Graph.

2. Before you begin, clear your mind of distractions. Now reflect briefly on the previous twenty-four hours. Consider the events of the day—what happened? What were your emotions, thoughts, and physical sensations?

3. Immediately fill in the Food and Body Feedback Graph to

create a visual record that reflects the past twenty-four hours.

4. Rate each of the following categories, giving them a value from one (horrible) to ten (terrific):

- Body: how I felt physically
- Mind: how I felt mentally
- Emotion: how I felt emotionally

Use a different color ink for each category. Day by day, connect the dots within each category. The object is to tap into your intuition by evaluating each category as quickly as possible—don't agonize over your answers. Instead, check in with your gut sense and immediately plot your responses.

PRACTICE: FEEDBACK EVALUATION SHEET

1. After you've gathered data for a week, lay out all of your Eating Record Charts side by side, in order from first day to last.
2. Now compare your Food and Body Feedback Graph to your Eating Record Charts. If there are any peaks or valleys in any of the lines on your Feedback Graph, look at your Eating Record Chart for the same day, as well as the day before. Do you have an intuitive sense that there was a correlation between what you ate, or other elements of your eating experi-

feedback evaluation sheet

MENU	PATTERNS
Any food you ate 6 times during the week?	
Any food you ate 10 times during the week?	
Any food you ate more than 10 times during the week?	
Any food you felt you ate a huge quantity of once or more?	

ACTIVITY	PATTERNS
How many times did you have snacks?	
How often did you eat somewhere other than at a dining table?	
How many times did you eat alone?	
How often did you do something (other than talking) besides simply eating during a meal or snack?	

HUNGER	PATTERNS
How many times were you hungry before you ate?	
How many times were you full when you finished eating?	

FEELINGS	PATTERNS
What emotions or physical feelings did you experience more than five times during the week?	

ence, and how you felt emotionally, physically, or mentally as reflected on your Feedback Graph? Make a note of anything that seems important in your journal.

3. Next, use the Feedback Evaluation Sheet. Go through each of the categories on the Eating Record Charts and answer the corresponding questions on the Feedback Evaluation Sheet. Tally them in the "Patterns" column.

4. Look for general, broad-based patterns. If, for example, you ate a salad for lunch every day and noticed that you had headaches before dinner, there may be a connection between lack of protein and your physical symptoms. Make a note in your journal of any pattern that piques your interest.

5. Over the next week, observe how these patterns come and go. Also observe, as you did in step 2, your intuitive sense of the relationship between your eating experience and how you feel: emotionally, physically, and mentally.

Reflection: If you've ever tracked your eating for diet programs, you've probably evaluated the data to see if you ate too much, ate fattening foods, or made poor choices. The patterns and insights that you should now look for have very little to do with these types of external concepts. We simply want to see what's actually going on. From this conscious perspective, you can see what throws you off balance, what may perpetuate your problem, and ways in which you keep yourself stuck. From this clear vantage point, you'll have the perspective you need to make lasting change.

PRACTICE: AWAKENING CONSCIOUS EATING

The practice of conscious eating is one way to connect to your personal sense of spirituality. Being conscious means that you are tapping into your core. The seemingly simple act of having the intention to stay conscious as you eat, and maintain attention to the process of eating, can completely alter your relationship with food. In this way, the act of eating becomes a vital link to your personal purpose.

The following practice introduces you to some basic techniques for conscious eating. It will help you to break food patterns that otherwise may feel powerful, overwhelming, destructive, or out of control.

1. Select a food that you enjoy the appearance and taste of, but one that doesn't hold conflict for you in any way. (Don't pick a food that you wrestle with, or one that you feel might make you lose control, such as a bag of potato chips, where you feel if you eat one, you'll eat them all. In Chapter Nine, we'll provide a strategy for dealing with foods that you feel you can't control.)

2. Choose a time when you can eat the food alone without being disturbed. Don't have the TV on or music playing, and don't read—let it be just you and the food, nothing else.

3. Place the food on the table and sit facing it. Take a moment to clear your mind and drink in the appearance and aroma of the food.

4. Before you eat, set the intention to focus your complete attention on the first and last bites of the food, and to note any feedback you receive as you eat. This sounds deceptively simple. Don't be surprised if it's challenging.

5. As your teeth sink into the first bite, try to slow down the moment so you experience it fully and consciously. When you finish chewing the bite, savor the sensations and listen to any feedback you may experience.

6. For the rest of the meal, eat as you normally would. But as you prepare to take the last bite, repeat the exercise that you did with the first bite, trying to focus all of your attention and to remain fully conscious.

7. After you've finished eating, take just a moment to write in your journal any information about the practice, your experience, and your feedback. Consider what percentage of time you were conscious between the first and last bites, and what percentage of time your thoughts were elsewhere. Did set-

ting your intention to remain conscious for the first and last bites make you more conscious in between, or just for those bites?

Reflection: The first time you try this practice, you may find that you can't manage to be conscious for the final bite. That's perfectly normal. It's much harder to remain aware of what we're doing for even a small period of time than it might seem at the outset.

Repeat this simple food practice once a day for a week. You may eat the same food or choose different foods each time. You'll probably notice that the amount of time you spend consciously aware of your food and the eating experience between bites will increase gradually over the week.

turning a practice into a way of life

The food practices are intended to help us find a new way of relating to eating, in order to replace old, destructive patterns of behavior with healthy ones. Controlling weight isn't the primary purpose of these practices, but once they start changing the way we relate to food, bringing our weight into balance can often be a welcome side effect.

This works very simply. By remaining conscious as we eat, we learn how to accurately interpret our internal feedback stream. We learn to listen to our body for signals about what and when we need to eat, so our eating behavior is no longer dictated by habit, theories, or diets. Conscious eating teaches us to acknowledge and respond appropriately to the voice of internal needs. Habitual eating patterns and behaviors are gradually replaced by hearing our feedback and responding to what we need in the moment.

The more we eat the foods our bodies actually need, the better we feel. This motivates us to want to tune into the messages from our body and feel better all the time.

SEVEN

moving into your own mind/body practice

"Home is the place where, when you have to go there,
They have to take you in."

—ROBERT FROST, "THE DEATH OF THE HIRED MAN"

We come home to a place that is our own. Home could be a house, a room, or a yard—anywhere we belong. Home is also a place within us, our own home base that we carry wherever we go in the world.

We know that place in our gut—where we are alone but not lonely. Whether we're surrounded by the din of humanity on a crowded city street, or are all by ourselves on top of a rock at the ocean's edge, we're at home when we are authentically being ourselves.

This place we call home is always inside of us, ready at any instant to welcome us in. It's both a sense of inner space and a feeling of being liberated from the normal sense of time and place—a space where time ceases to matter. It's a sacred realm where there's no desire to be anyone other than precisely who you are, and to let everything that surrounds you be precisely what it is. When you're there you feel passionate, vibrant, and alive with the excitement of having woken up in the middle of your life into the present moment. In this place or state of being, you are yourself *right now*.

As we said earlier in the book, to initiate change, we must start from where we are—"Home is where one starts from." But if home is so pleasurable and always available to us, why aren't we always there? And more important, how do we get there from where we are right now?

Author Ray Bradbury once said that mankind doesn't go to outer space to find aliens; mankind goes to outer space to discover himself. All of us must at some point leave behind our childhood homes and families to create our own adult lives and forge our own identities. But as time goes by, we may find it increasingly difficult to return home (both literally and metaphorically) and rediscover where we started from. The paradox is that we must go out into the world to discover our own unique nature. But the danger is that, on our journey, we may lose ourselves forever.

The mind/body practices that we're about to engage in are road maps for finding your way back home. Mind/body practices cultivate an awareness of our own inner space, our home base. The practices facilitate our ability within that space to listen to our sense of personal purpose and to our feedback.

But when we return home for the long-awaited reunion, we may not find it an experience of pure unadulterated bliss. What we'll find in our home is the sum total of *all* of our life's experiences: our history, memories, habitual perceptions, and responses.

Even though being at home is an experience of true happiness, not everything that arises there is pleasant. To be present with *everything* that makes up the "you" right now, in this moment, can be painful. The shame from memories of words misspoken, the dull throb of a headache, harsh judgments, or self-criticism are among the many painful sensations, thoughts, and feelings that reside alongside the pleasant ones. So we may avoid going home because to truly be there means experiencing all of yourself: the good, the bad, *and* the ugly.

Mind/body practices can help us to deal with the difficulties that may arise in going home. The practices allow us to perceive our most familiar thoughts, actions, or sensations in a brand-new way. To really see something as it is in the present moment, you have to drop your preconceptions. Everything you encounter is something brand-new, never experienced until *right now*.

Although a "Rose is a rose is a rose," each flower from the same bush has its own unique character and presentation. Even the same blossom changes drastically over time. So to be at home, to be present, we must be awake to see that all things are uniquely different and all things are bound to change. Home is our harbor in the storm, a still place from which we can safely observe the tumultuous constant change that is our lives.

homeward bound

The first step to getting home from where we are is to develop the ability to consciously observe our present state. Fortunately, there's no need to reinvent the wheel here. Traditional Eastern mind/body practices, such as yoga and meditation, cultivate mindfulness and the experience of the present moment. These practices have grown out of rich philosophical traditions that are thousands of years old, driven by people's desire to understand the meaning of life and the self.

The goal of the mind/body practices is to integrate mind and body, bringing us naturally into a state of holistic awareness.

Mind/body practices are composed of a set structure, such as a yoga pose that's held for five breaths, or a meditation posture that's held for fifteen minutes. This structure can become a sacred space within which you can safely experiment and explore.

Mind/body practices put us in touch with our breath, connecting us with the sensations, thoughts, and emotions we're currently experiencing. Breath reveals and illuminates everything it comes in contact with in our bodies, and it focuses our attention. In a mind/body practice, we also direct our eyes to a single point, again to help focus attention.

Fixing our gaze and being conscious of our breath allows us to move with awareness grounded from our core. Moving from this internal connection to our center, we wake up to deeper and deeper levels of feedback.

We bring both intention and attention to the practice. As we repeat the practices over time, we pay attention to sensations and feelings that arise, maintaining the intention to return to the present moment whenever the mind, breath, or gaze wanders. The consistency and repetition of the practices help us to find our way back home.

The following yoga practice serves as an introduction to how mind/body practices work. It combines postures from various yoga traditions and is constructed to give you a feeling for the rhythmical flow and transforming effects of a mind/body practice.

moving into your own mind/body practice

Once you start to experience the benefits of the yoga practice, you may consider looking for a teacher to advise you on how to broaden and deepen your practice. Practices are traditionally learned from a teacher who can help you overcome your limitations and keep you challenged. If no teachers are available locally, or you can't find one you relate to, try a good video or book. You may also consider finding a workshop with a known teacher. For more recommendations, see Suggested Readings.

PRACTICE: A BEGINNER'S YOGA PRACTICE

When mindfulness is brought into the body in action, the effects can be profound. This yoga practice helps you experience your own internal home, where you make the choices that determine your actions.

basics:

1. For the yoga practice to have an optimal effect, it's best to do it daily. If this seems too much of a time commitment, you can practice less often. Fewer than two practice sessions a week, however, won't maintain the continuity needed for you to start making ongoing changes. But start where you are and work your way from there: once a week is

101

better than never, and five minutes is better than nothing.

2. Start by setting your intention—why you're doing this yoga practice and what you hope to get out of it. Return to your intention often during the practice, whenever your mind wanders or you become distracted.

3. As you begin moving and using your body in new ways, you may experience some initial muscle soreness. But as you continue to practice, you'll notice the movements becoming easier to master, and your body getting stronger and more supple.

4. To see the effects of the practice—both in how easily you can perform the moves and the overall changes you're experiencing—it's good to look at your progress over time. Though sometimes you may feel that you're stuck and nothing is changing, you'll be able to appreciate your progress when you look back.

setting a time for your practice: It's good to practice at approximately the same time each day in order to establish a routine. When you practice at a set time, you're more likely to regard the practice as a part of your daily routine and plan around it, rather than attempting to squeeze it into your already busy life. If you can't set a regular time to practice, any time will do. The key is to try to do the practice at least twice a week, with energy, concentration, and enough time that you don't feel rushed.

defining a space for your practice:

1. Choose a room that's quiet, spacious enough that you don't feel restricted in movement, and one in which you can be alone. Make this your regular practice space so that you don't spend your time wandering around looking for the "right" peaceful spot.
2. A noncarpeted surface is best because your feet and body can be more evenly supported without wobbling. If you have only carpeted rooms, don't let that stop you; any flat surface will do to get you started.
3. A yoga "sticky mat" rolled out onto the floor gives you good traction and support. If you don't want to buy a sticky mat, you may use a thin, rubber-backed carpet piece or a nonslippery blanket.
4. Keep the temperature of the room comfortably warm. Heat is greatly beneficial for warming up and helping you feel limber so you can relax into the poses.

what to wear:

1. Wear comfortable clothing. Loose-fitting shorts and a T-shirt, or leotard and leggings, are ideal. Avoid clothes that bind or bunch up as you move.
2. It's essential to have bare feet so you can use your feet to grip the surface of the sticky mat or floor.

when and what to eat: Some people find that they practice better on an empty stomach; others can eat a light meal or snack shortly before practice. A general rule of thumb is to give yourself three to four hours after a large meal before you practice.

Don't deprive yourself of the food you need simply to have an empty stomach when you practice. Otherwise, you could find yourself dizzy, weak, and unable to complete your practice. Experiment with what works for you.

general guidelines for each pose:

1. Before beginning your yoga practice, set your intention to continually return to the present moment during the practice.
2. Allow the movements of the postures to feel as if they generate from your core.
3. Attempt to engage only the muscles needed to execute the

104

movement of each pose. We often seem to try holding a posture with our face, tightening our jaw, knitting our brow, and the like. So make sure to relax your face, tongue, and palate (roof of the mouth) as you move and hold the poses.

4. The yoga postures feel much more natural and graceful if you open your heart—literally stretching wide the whole chest area at the level of your heart. In doing this, be careful not to overly curve your lower back. Try to open up from the inside, both front and back.

5. As you breathe in and out through your nose, partially close your glottis (the back of your throat) so that the breath makes a soft, aspirant sound, as if you were whispering. The resulting sound helps you to focus your attention and move from your core.

6. Breathe smooth, full, deep breaths that are comfortable. Keep your mouth relaxed and your lips closed as you breathe. If you notice uneven breathing, refocus your mind by returning to your initial intention to stay present, and bring your attention to the feelings and sensations within.

7. Coordinate your movements with the breath, almost as if the breath itself moves the pose.

8. Keep your gaze steady and soft during each pose. It's helpful to choose a gazing point on which to fix your eyes. Even

though you have your eyes open, looking outward, your actual focus and attention is fixed within.

9. Arrange your sticky mat or carpet so that it is square with the room. If it's askew, it can distract you visually and make you feel off balance even if you're not.

10. In general, never strain in the postures to attain your "ideal" of the outer form. Recognize the limitations of *your* body. At the same time, explore the edge of your flexibility and strength. There's a fine line between wise caution and energetic experimentation. Approach it mindfully.

STANDING

1. Stand at the front end of your sticky mat with your feet together and the sides of your big toes touching. Allow your arms to hang comfortably at your sides as you keep your heart open and your shoulders back. Stand straight and tall with your eyes closed and your feet planted evenly on the floor as if they're rooted into the ground. As you release your tongue, palate, and facial muscles, focus on the internal

feeling of balance. Feel the center of the crown of your head lifting, helping you to draw up the center of your body. Allow the breath to flow in and out, smoothly and deeply, never straining but maintaining an even course.

2. Stay in the pose for twenty smooth, easy breaths, watching the flow of the breath as it moves in and out, bringing a sense of calm and balance to the pose.

ARMS OVER HEAD

1. As you stand, spread your toes and ground your feet, arms hanging comfortably at your side. Gaze gently straight ahead. Take several deep, calm breaths.

2. Take a full breath in, then release. Turn your palms out, and with the next inhale, reach up over your head with your arms held long and straight. Feel the sensation of your back relaxing and spreading and your shoulders dropping away from your ears. Look up at your fingertips.

3. Reach high while still grounding through the soles of your feet. Then exhale, bringing your hands slowly back down to your sides and lowering your head so that you're looking

straight ahead. Eventually you'll be able to touch your hands above your head without crunching your shoulders or neck. Work toward this, but don't sacrifice the grace of the movement simply to reach the goal of touching your hands overhead.

4. Repeat this movement slowly five times, coordinating the raising of the arms and head with the inhale, and the lowering of the arms and head with the exhale.

BENDING FORWARD

1. Stand straight and tall, with your feet about hip width apart. Have your arms down by your sides and your shoulders rolled back as you ground through the soles of your feet. Gaze straight ahead and open your heart, bringing your attention to the core of your body. Take two smooth breaths.

2. With the next inhale, place your hands on your hips. With the exhale, begin to fold forward, keeping your back straight. As you bend, gently look up slightly. Fold only as far forward as you can while still keeping your back straight.

Keep your legs straight and your kneecaps lifting as you fold. If you feel stiff, you may bend your knees.

3. Shift your gaze down along the line of your nose. Once forward, place your hands on your thighs, shins, or the floor (depending on how far over you've folded). Release your spine so that you're hanging in a comfortable fold. Take five full breaths, releasing into the pose little by little on each exhale.

4. At the end of the last breath, put your hands on your hips and, with the inhale, return to standing, straightening your back as you lift up.

SIMPLE TRIANGLE POSE

1. Turn sideways on your mat and spread your feet parallel, three and a half to four feet apart, with approximately one leg length between your feet. Turn your right foot so that it's perpendicular to your left foot. Turn your right knee all the

way out to the side so it's facing the same direction as your toes. Turn your left foot in at about a 45-degree angle. Your right heel should align with the front edge of your left heel. Stabilize the pose by spreading your toes and grounding your feet evenly.

2. Place your hands on your hips. Lift your head, relax your palate, and open your heart as you bring your shoulders back. Gaze gently straight ahead.

3. Take two breaths as you find balance in the pose.

4. Take a deep breath in. At the top of the inhale, tilt your hips to the right and begin to exhale. As you fold slowly over, move your upper body out over your right leg. Keep your gaze steady and your head in line with your spine. As you bend, continue to lengthen through the crown of your head and ground through your feet while lifting your kneecaps. Try to keep your upper body straight and evenly positioned over your right leg.

5. Hold the pose for five breaths. At the end of the last exhale, ground your feet and straighten back up to standing.

6. Now turn your left foot out and right foot in and repeat the pose on the other side. Return to standing.

LUNGE POSE

1. Stand near the front of your mat with your feet together. Bend forward, placing your fingertips on the floor at shoulder width, beside your feet. If you can't reach the floor with your hands and keep your legs straight, bend your knees. On an exhale, step back with your left leg into a lunge position. If you can, flatten your hands and ground them evenly. Step onto the ball of your left foot, placing it about three to four feet away from your right foot.

2. Straighten your left leg as much as possible. Open your heart and widen your back as you square and drop your shoulders. Hold this position for five breaths.

3. Drop your left knee down onto the floor. Bring your right knee back so that you're on all fours. Place the ball of your right foot on the floor, and bring your left foot up between your hands. Hold the lunge on this side for five breaths.

4. Drop your right knee down to the ground and bring your left knee back so that you're on all fours again. Sit back on your heels, and slowly return to standing.

BALANCING

1. While learning how to get your balance, you may wish to stand close to a wall or a piece of furniture so that you can hold on. For easiest balance, stand on the bare floor with your feet slightly separated. Gaze straight ahead and take two full breaths.

2. On an inhale, place your hands on your hips. Straighten your spine and lift gently through the crown of your head as you exhale. Shift your weight to your left foot. Carefully ground the foot by spreading the toes and distributing the weight evenly over the sole.

3. On another inhale, bend your right knee and slide your foot up the inside of your left leg. Use your right hand to help lift and place your foot on the inner top of your left thigh. When you feel stable, let go of your foot and return your hand to your hip.

4. Balance here for five breaths. Don't lock and hyperextend your left knee; allow it to remain strong yet relaxed. Fix your gaze on a point at eye level or on the floor several feet in

front of you. Make sure to breathe! On an exhale, lower the right leg to standing and redistribute your weight evenly between your feet.

5. Repeat the balance on the other side, standing this time on your right leg.

WALL DOG

1. Face an empty wall, standing about two feet away with your feet hip distance apart. Place your hands, shoulder width apart, at shoulder height on the wall. Spread your hands, middle fingers pointing straight up toward the ceiling.

2. Step back and slide your hands down the wall until your back is perpendicular to the floor. Keep your legs straight and your hands slightly higher than your head. Relax your head and drop it between your arms. Stay here for five breaths.

3. After your last exhale, inhale as you walk your hands back up the wall until you're standing. Rest here, finding your balance for two breaths.

HALF DOWNWARD DOG

1. Come down on all fours. Slide your hands forward so that your arms are straight out in front of you as you lean forward and place your forehead on the floor. Keep your thighs vertical and point your toes so that the tops of your feet are resting on the floor. Close your eyes and stretch. Breathe.

2. Extend and straighten your spine by reaching up and back through your sitting bones, and slightly down and forward through your forehead. Keep your arms straight, shoulders back, armpits and wrists gently lifting away from the floor.

3. Remain in this position for five breaths. On an inhale, fold your knees and sit back, leaving your head on the floor. After two full breaths, sit up.

SPHINX

1. Lie belly-down on your mat with your legs together and your arms along your sides. Rest your forehead on the floor and take two full breaths.

2. Crawl up onto your elbows, hands pointing out in front of you. Lift your head and chest. Slide your elbows so that they're directly under your shoulders. Your fingers should be spread and pointing forward, your forearms parallel, and your wrists pressing flat into the floor. Gaze straight ahead.

3. Pause here for five breaths, breathing fully and slowly. Press into the floor with your elbows, forearms, wrists, and hands, allowing both the front and back of your rib cage to expand and your shoulders to spread and drop back. Keep your legs straight and slightly engaged.

4. During the last exhale, return your forehead to the floor. Close your eyes and draw your arms back straight along the sides of your body. Rest here for two breaths, breathing into any residual sensations.

REPETITION

Repeat the Sphinx and then the Half Downward Dog two more times each before moving on to the next pose.

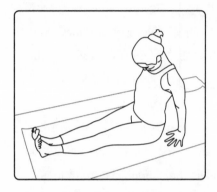

STAFF

1. Sit with your legs stretched straight out in front of you. Place your hands on the floor, palms down, just slightly behind your buttocks. Your fingertips should be facing forward and your arms straight. If you're stiff, try moving your arms farther back behind you.

2. Flex your feet and reach out through the bottoms of your heels to straighten your legs. Lower your head slightly and look down. Keep the integrity of the pose with your back and arms straight, your shoulders back, and your legs reaching. Hold the pose for five breaths, then release.

SITTING FORWARD BEND

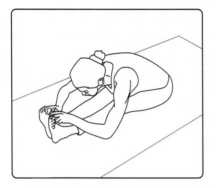

1. Again sit with your back straight and your legs stretched out in front of you. Rock from one side to the other, and pull the skin of your buttocks out to the side so that you're sitting as flat as possible. (If your back curves and you can't sit straight, or if you can't straighten your legs, place a firm pillow or folded blanket under your sitting bones. Elevate yourself until you can sit comfortably straight.) Flex your feet and reach out through the bottom of your heels to straighten your legs. Don't roll your legs out—keep your kneecaps pointing straight up. Sit in this position for five breaths.

2. On an inhale, reach your arms up overhead, stretching. At the end of the inhale, begin to fold forward, bending from your hips, and exhale, reaching for your toes. Keep your heart open, shoulders dropping away from your ears, and legs straight. (If it's difficult to keep your legs straight, check to see that you're sufficiently elevated. You may also bend your knees; be certain to do so if you have any pain in your back.)

3. Come only as far forward as feels comfortable. If you can't hold your big toes with your fingers, loop a strap or belt around the outside of your feet, just below the ball of the foot. Then hold the strap and gently pull. Gradually straighten your legs, pushing the inner edge and base of each big toe forward. Hold the pose for five breaths. On an inhale, release and sit back up.

FOOT-TO-KNEE FORWARD BEND

1. Sit straight with your legs stretched out. If your back is curved, elevate your hips with a cushion or blanket. Bend your right knee out to the side. Place your right foot on the inside of your left thigh, as close to the top of the thigh as possible. If your right knee doesn't rest comfortably on the floor, prop it up with a cushion.

2. On an inhale, reach your arms up overhead, stretching. At the end of the inhale, begin to fold forward, bending from your hips. Exhale, reaching for the toes of your left foot. Keep your heart open, shoulders dropping away from your ears, and legs straight.

3. Bend only as far forward as you can without straining your back or your hip joints. If you can't reach your toes, loop a belt or strap around your foot and pull on it to bring you forward. Try to keep your left foot flexed and vertical. Rest in this forward bend for five breaths.

4. On an inhale, sit up and straighten both legs out. Bring your left foot into the top of your right thigh and repeat the posture on the opposite side.

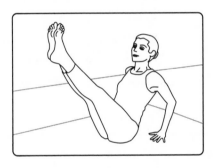

BOAT

1. Sit with your knees bent and your feet flat on the floor. Support yourself with your hands on the floor behind you, about shoulder distance apart, fingers facing forward. Keep your back as straight as possible, sitting bones rolling forward. Gaze gently down. Rest in this position for two breaths.

2. After exhaling, lift your feet and straighten your legs so they're at about a 45-degree angle from the floor. You may need to lean back slightly into your arms as you raise your feet, but then work forward, shifting the weight out of your arms onto the edge of your sitting bones. Stay in this position with your heart lifted and your shoulders dropping down and back. Gaze at your toes for five breaths. Release and rest for a breath, then repeat the pose twice more.

COBBLER'S POSE

1. Starting out in a seated position, put the soles of your feet together and bend your knees so that they point out to the sides. Hold your feet with your hands. Move your feet so that the soles are together, toes pointing away from you. As in the sitting forward bend, if you can't keep your back straight and sitting bones grounded, elevate yourself on a pillow or blankets.

2. Draw your feet in toward your body so that they're three to twelve inches away. Gaze steadily ahead. Release your hip muscles and press down toward the floor with your knees so that the sides of your legs approach the floor. Stay in this position for five breaths.

SPINAL TWIST

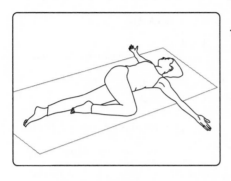

1. Lie on your back looking up with your legs straight. Stretch your arms out to the side at shoulder height, palms down on the floor. Take two full breaths, stretching down through your feet and up through the crown of your head.

2. Inhaling, draw your right knee up and place your right foot on your left knee. On the exhale, roll your hips to the left side, folding your right knee down toward the floor outside of your left knee. Keep your left leg straight and your arms reaching out. Your right arm may come away from the floor, but keep your right shoulder down on the ground. Rest in this twist for five breaths.

3. On the next inhale, roll back up and straighten your right leg. Repeat the twist on the other side, this time with your left knee bent, rolling to the right. Repeat the twist twice more on each side.

BRIDGE SHOULDER STAND

1. Lie on your back. Inhaling, bend your knees and place your feet flat on the floor with your heels almost touching your hips. You should be able to touch your ankles with your fingertips, but don't grasp them; let your arms lie flat. Drop your shoulders back and relax your neck, resting your head evenly on the floor. Take two breaths in this position.

2. At the end of an exhale, begin to lift your hips straight up, away from the floor. Push through your feet and keep your thighs parallel to each other. Walk your shoulders down and back. Interlace your fingers behind your back. Straighten your arms out along the floor and keep your neck relaxed. Allow the chest to move toward your chin, keeping your heart open, but don't move your chin to your chest! Hold the pose for five breaths, then lower your hips to the floor, placing your sacrum on the floor last. Unlace your fingers as you lower your hips.

BENT-KNEES TWIST

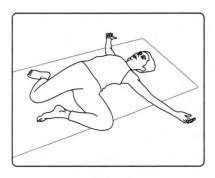

1. Remain on your back with your knees bent. Shift your feet slightly away from your hips so they're resting on the edges of your sticky mat, about eighteen inches apart.

2. Spread your arms out along the floor at shoulder height with your palms up. On an exhale, lower both knees toward the floor to the right side of your mat. Keep the upper part of your back flat on the floor by reaching out with your arms and allowing the lower part of your spine to twist. Hold this position for three breaths.

3. On an inhale, raise both knees together, then lower them to the left side as you exhale. Again, keep your back open and flattening toward the floor as you twist. After five breaths, raise both knees to the center on an inhale.

4. Repeat this twist five times on each side. After the last twist, straighten your legs out along the floor and rest on your back for two full breaths.

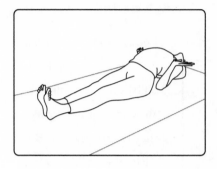

FISH

1. Straighten your legs so you're lying flat on your back with your arms along your sides. Reach out through your heels and take two breaths.

2. Pressing through your elbows, lift your chest on an inhale as you rock forward slightly with your hips. Moving out from the spine, roll your head backward so that the top back part of your head rests comfortably on the floor. Then gaze gently down your nose.

3. On the next inhale, press down through your elbows to help you open your heart and expand the lift in your chest. Exhale as you slide your fingers under your hips. Position your hips so the sitting bones are square and tilting down toward the floor.

4. Continue to push into the floor with your elbows, and reposition for maximum stretch. Draw your fingers out from beneath your hips, leaving your elbows on the ground and holding your hands away from your sides. Rest in this position for five breaths.

5. To come out of the pose, drop your hands to the floor. Take more weight into your elbows and lift your head up away

from the floor. Straighten your neck and gently lower yourself back down to a flat position. Rest here for two breaths.

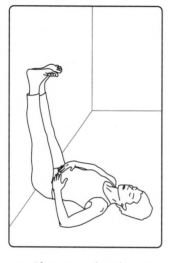

FEET UP THE WALL

1. Move your mat so that it's flush
   with the baseboard of an empty
   wall. Lie on your back with your
   hips as close to the wall as possible. Raise your legs up the wall,
   keeping them straight and together, so that your legs and upper body form a right angle.

2. Place your hands on your lower belly and close your eyes.
   Rest in this position for at least ten breaths. Bend your knees
   and roll over gently to the side to come out of the pose.

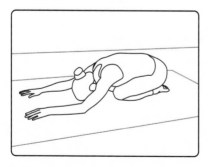

CHILD'S POSE

1. Crawl onto all fours. Sit
   back onto your heels,
   bending fully at the hips.
   Leave your hands on the
   floor, arms outstretched,

and place your forehead on the floor between your elbows.

2. Relax. Rest in this position for at least ten breaths with your eyes closed.

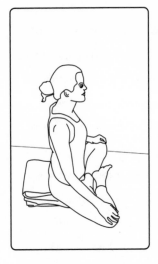

SITTING

1. Sit on the floor with your legs crossed in front of you and your back straight. Don't strain your legs or knees. As in the Cobbler's Pose, place a blanket or cushion under your sitting bones if necessary to help tilt your pelvis so that your back is straight.

2. Rest your hands on your lap or knees and close your eyes. Move your shoulders back and down, and lift up through the crown of your head to get the sense that your torso is floating. Stay in this position for twenty breaths.

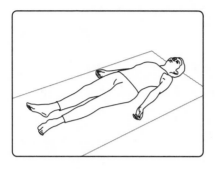

CORPSE

1. Lie flat on your back with your eyes closed and legs together, reaching out through your heels. Allow your shoulders to drop back and down into the floor, as your body relaxes and melts. Allow your feet to fall away from each other and your breath to become smooth and steady. Stay here for at least twenty-five breaths, or until your body feels calm and relaxed. Take up to ten minutes in this pose if you'd like.

2. After you're finished, take several deep breaths, then begin to slowly move your fingers and toes. Stretch your arms out overhead and stretch out through your legs. Draw your legs up one at a time, and roll gently to your right side, resting your head on your arm. Then roll all the way over to the Child's Pose and rest here for five breaths. Slowly sit up, and rest in a sitting position for at least ten breaths to end your practice for the day.

PRACTICE: TRADITIONAL SITTING MEDITATION—
PLEASURE AND PAIN

This sitting meditation, like the Walking Meditation practice we learned in Chapter Four (see page 59), is derived from the Buddhist Vipassana tradition. We've adapted it to focus on observing the two opposite poles that dominate so much of our existence: pleasure and pain.

Buddhism teaches that we suffer because of our desire to grasp onto pleasurable experiences and push away painful ones. We run with open arms toward the good stuff and run away at high speed from the bad. But our very desire for pleasure is what causes our pain, because it's painful not to get what we want. In a world of constant change, even when we get what we want, that pleasure must end sooner or later. The loss of this pleasure causes us pain. Similarly, whatever is painful will also pass, bringing with it the possibility for further pleasure.

This sitting practice allows you to observe pain and pleasure, watching both move through your mind without getting caught up and carried away by either. As you observe how painful sensations come and go, you realize that your pain isn't a solid unchanging mass. Rather, it's something that's constantly transforming and changing. It has no real or permanent existence. Similarly, you watch pleasurable sensations flit in and out of your mind. Instead of grasping on to them, you simply observe your desire to hold onto pleasure.

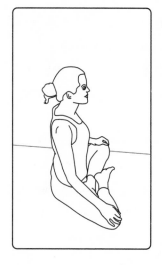

getting seated:

1. Start by sitting in a comfortable position, preferably on the floor. The best position is one that allows your legs and knees to remain comfortable as you sit over a period of time. Sitting on the floor is traditional, and it induces an energetic physical state, as well as a contemplative state of mind.

2. However, for many of us, sitting on the floor in this way is not comfortable or even possible. A good variation is to sit on the floor with your back supported by a wall. This can help to hold up your body, keep your back straight and comfortable, and take the pressure off your legs and knees. If this also proves too uncomfortable, a couch or a chair will do. Sitting comfortably—whether on the floor or in a chair—is essential if you're to stick with this practice. Therefore, err on the side of comfort!

3. If you do choose to sit on the floor, many people prefer a

combination of mats and cushions in order to sit comfortably over an extended period of time. Generally, you want your knees to be touching the ground. That may mean sitting on the edge of a cushion, which puts your body at the proper angle for your knees to reach the ground, and for your back to be upright and straight. If your knees still don't comfortably rest on the ground, try using a prop underneath your knees (like a pillow).

4. It's also helpful to sit on a padded surface, such as a carpet, cushion, or blanket, so that your ankles won't become sore as they rest on the floor. Try experimenting with various combinations of cushions, blankets, and pillows to find what works best for your body.

when and where:

1. As with the yoga practice, doing your sitting practice at the same time each day is helpful to make it a part of your routine. However, if this isn't practical, do it when you can; just build it into your schedule on a daily basis.

2. Forty-five minutes is an ideal amount of time for sitting, but if you find that too difficult to begin with, try building up your stamina. Start with ten minutes, and increase it every week by five more minutes until you reach forty-five min-

utes. Again, just ten minutes of meditating is better than nothing!

3. It's preferable not to have eaten before sitting. An empty stomach is more physically comfortable, and it helps prevent the sleepiness that often follows a meal.

4. These are just recommended guidelines. Finding the time to do both a yoga and sitting practice within your very busy schedule might seem difficult. If so, alternate the practices during the week.

5. Ultimately, how long and how often you sit is up to you. The main goal is to find a sustainable framework for a sitting practice that works with who you are and with your lifestyle. That way, you'll be able to reap the benefits and stick with it.

6. If it's possible, try setting aside a space in your home where you can do both your yoga and sitting practice—your quiet space, your "home" inside your house. Make sure that you've also set aside practice times during which you won't be interrupted.

going inside:

1. Once you're seated comfortably, close your eyes. Start by noticing any sounds you may hear, such as external noise: a radio in the background, cars going by on the street. Internal

noise is more often subtle and delicate: the buzzing in your ears, or a primordial sound that you can hear if you listen very closely and deeply—the hum of your existence.

2. Next, start noticing your breath as it moves in and out. Breathe through your nose. Unlike our work with the breath in yoga, there's no attempt to control the breath in sitting meditation. You simply observe the breath as it takes its own course in and out. Notice the different qualities of each breath—soft, strong, smooth, strained, warm, cool, fast, slow. Just watch with no expectations as to how each breath will or should unfold. Let your attention come to rest in a particular place (tip of your nose, chest, abdomen). This will help steady your attention.

3. To focus your attention and help you stay conscious, you may also find it useful to make a mental notation that quickly names what you're observing. For instance, if it helps you to observe your breath with greater concentration, you could note an inhaling breath as "rising" or just "in," and an exhaling breath as "falling" or "out." Experiment to see if labeling in this way seems to help focus your attention, or if it distracts you. Leave it out if you find it distracting.

4. As soon as your focus on your breath is interrupted by thoughts, notice that you're thinking. Observe the process instead of becoming lost in the thoughts. Whatever your

thoughts are—grocery lists, judgments, fantasies, vacation plans, memories—let them come up and observe them. Again, you may find it useful to note "thinking" as these thoughts arise. By the time you become aware of the fact that you're thinking, you may have been doing so for a very long time! That's perfectly normal. As soon as we're aware that we've been lost in thought, we have an immediate opportunity to return to mindfulness. Our awareness is our link to consciousness.

5. When thinking no longer dominates your attention, return to observing the breath. There's no value placed on observing breath rather than thoughts. In this practice, you just notice whatever's taking center stage and demanding your attention at any given moment.

6. As you meditate, you'll also start to notice physical sensations, feelings of hot, cold, tingling, itching, burning, aching, tickling. As these sensations arise and come to the forefront of your attention, make them the object of your observation. Again, if it's helpful, acknowledge the sensation with a quick mental note—"heat," "cold," "tingling." As soon as a sensation is no longer the predominant focus of your attention, return to observing the breath.

7. Now start to notice emotions or mental states as they arise: feelings of fear, anger, sadness, happiness, regret, anticipa-

tion, anxiety, love. Use the noting process if it helps you to focus your awareness—"happy," "sad," "confused." As the emotions are perceived and then pass, return gently to observing the breath. (*Note:* When a strong emotion is present, try to notice what you're experiencing physically. Often there's a physical correlation to emotion.)

8. Be alert and observant as sounds, thoughts, physical sensations, and emotions rise and pass. In sitting meditation, it's as if your mind is observing a filmstrip going by, frame by frame, a movie that goes on without end. In every given moment, the film advances another frame, and you as the audience merely watch. Be alert to each new frame as it first comes on the screen. Pay attention so that you can observe as it fades away and the next frame moves in.

9. On all of these levels—sound, thought, physical sensations, and emotions—we experience pleasure and pain. As we sit, we may experience physical discomfort—our knee, back, or neck is hurting. Or we may discover that it feels great to sit, we're so happy to be still and peaceful that we feel great pleasure. Similarly, we may find the process of observing sound, breath, thoughts, sensations, or feelings either pleasurable or painful.

10. Start to observe your tendency to embrace the pleasurable

experiences: "This feeling of peace and happiness is what meditation is all about! I love sitting here and having these beautiful feelings!" Then notice how you push away the painful experiences: "Why does *my* back have to ache? I want to return to that wonderful peaceful feeling I had a few moments ago!" Our innate tendency to push away pain and embrace pleasure is fundamentally human. It's nothing to be ashamed or proud of, it's just how we are. But it also keeps us caught in the trap of desiring happy things and rejecting unpleasant things. Learning how to neither grasp nor push away pain and pleasure can teach us how to find the peace that can sustain us through both poles of experience. We can start waking up to whatever is *our* lot right now, and find a mode of peaceful acceptance.

11. When a painful feeling arises, instead of simply noting it as pain, take a more exploratory attitude—what are the sensations you're actually experiencing? Is it burning, prickling, tingling, sharp, throbbing; does it feel expansive or contracted; is it hot or cold? Act as if you've never experienced this sensation before, and truly question its nature with an open mind.

12. Try bringing your breath into the area that's feeling painful, and use it to open up the pain and observe it.

Often, you discover that the sensation you labeled as "pain" dissolves and goes away. The trick is, if you're observing pain in this way simply to make it go away, then you're back in the habitual position of trying to escape. But if you bring your breath to the sensation as an earnest inquiry, you'll be able to observe the process of change and transformation of the pain. You'll discover that your pain isn't a solid unchanging mass but a phenomenon of sensation that passes as you experience its temporary nature.

13. It's also important to note that there's a distinction between temporary pain, which passes, and real pain caused by sitting incorrectly or in a posture longer than your body can sustain. A good rule of thumb for distinguishing is to note if the pain doesn't go away after you've finished sitting, when you've had a chance to walk around a bit to work out the kinks. If you have lasting pain after sitting, consider changing your posture. Or try using one of the more supportive sitting postures described above, such as sitting in a chair or up against a wall.

14. As you did with pain, observe your reaction toward pleasant experiences. Try to watch these pleasant experiences without running away with them, which causes you to

lose your mindful awareness. Rather than just noting "pleasure," describe what is pleasurable—is it a pleasurable thought, sensation, or emotion? As with pain, remaining observant and not losing yourself in the pleasure is a major challenge. We long to run away with pleasure and achieve a few moments of happiness. Again, there's nothing wrong with this tendency—it's quite human, and of course quite pleasurable! But in this practice, we want to learn how to observe and identify personally with whatever arises and passes.

Reflection: Practicing meditation teaches us to recognize what makes up our existence from moment to moment. By learning how to observe instead of acting blindly, we gain the ability to choose our actions. Meditation deepens our insight into what it means to be alive, as we actively observe in any given moment the things we do, think, and feel.

When we learn not to jump at pleasure or run away from pain, we reap freedom from the automated response to each. We buy ourselves some time and space to consider with a fresh perspective what actions will bring us lasting happiness.

By practicing meditation in combination with yoga, we can train our bodies and minds to work together and create mindfulness in action. Although either meditation or yoga can work alone, both practiced together are complementary and speed up the process of positive change.

kicking the habit

The force of habit is powerful. Most of our lives are spent preferring one thought to another, one action to another, merely out of habit. Most of our food and body problems are maintained because we act automatically. We may try quite enthusiastically to find new solutions to our problems. But when we're bogged down by a lifetime of habit, getting unstuck can be elusive.

What's so slippery about trying to change our patterns is that we can't see precisely what we're doing most of the time. We know that we always seem to fall back into certain patterns of behavior. But we can't seem to figure out how it happens over and over again when we're trying so hard to apply our willpower and make changes.

The mind/body practices are designed to help us discover and resolve our habits. When we practice, we create a unique opportunity to simply observe our patterns, just watching and getting to know them.

When a habit emerges outside the realm of practice, it's usually as we're fully engaged in it—we yell at our spouse about the dirty dishes in the sink, we quickly open the cupboard and shove a snack in our mouths, or we glance in the mirror in disgust as we run out the door to work. We're acting without consciousness—that's how habits work.

At best, we may notice for an instant how we repeat this habit umpteen times. It reemerges because it comes from a pattern ingrained deep within. We've lost the ability to see it because it's so deeply etched in the darkness of our unconscious.

When we're doing our mind/body practices, we can just watch the habit emerge instead of having to engage in it. For example, this habitual thought might drift into your mind: "I'm such a fat pig!" But this time we're fully conscious of the words, hearing them and observing the painful judgment. We no longer run down another blind alley with the thoughts, feelings, and sensations that come up. In a mindful practice we observe and get to know those thoughts, feelings, and sensations.

Habits can grow like an unfettered fungus in the darkness of your unconscious and can take on an undue power because they don't have to withstand the light of day. Judgments and habits transform in the light of your consciousness quite naturally. They lose their disproportionate power when you see them for what they are.

In this way, a mind/body practice can completely change your life. You can learn to observe and know the unconscious habits and patterns that have been ruling your existence. You'll start to truly know yourself, the complete you, not just the partial picture that's available without mindfulness. Thinking and acting consciously is the ultimate freedom of truly being at home.

EIGHT

deepening your food practice

*No sooner had the warm liquid mixed with the crumbs touched my palate than a shud-
der ran through me and I stopped, intent upon the extraordinary thing that was happening to me . . . this new sensation having had on me the effect which love has of
filling me with a precious essence; or rather this essence was not in me, it was me.*

—MARCEL PROUST, *SWANN'S WAY*

sleight of hand

The fascination of a magic trick lies in the magician's skill at creating illusion. First the magician wins the audience's confidence by

assuring them of his trustworthiness ("Nothing up my sleeve!"). And then the trick begins. He shows you a deck of cards and gets you focused on the many details—the numbers, the suits, the order, and so on. Perhaps the magician has someone in the audience hold on to a card or shuffle the deck. While you're watching these complicated particulars, the magician is playing a completely different trick on you—he does indeed have that card up his sleeve.

This is exactly how a woman's food and body conflict is created and sustained, but we're the magicians tricking ourselves. We become ensnared in this magical illusion by buying into some or all of the underlying assumptions of the Covenant:

1. There is a right way and a wrong way to look, and the right way is supermodel-thin.
2. All women should want to be supermodel-thin.
3. The path to thinness is dieting, exercise, or any other number of externally directed methods of weight control.
4. Follow these decrees, and thinness and beauty can be yours forever.
5. You can have it all forever and ever—being thin and having the right look ensures happiness and bliss throughout eternity.

So we start at step one—"I should be thin! I must be thin! I will do anything to be thin!" And then we follow on through the next steps, trying to reach an elusive goal that never seems to stay within our grasp. "I just can't keep the weight off!" or "I'm twenty pounds under my ideal weight, starving myself successfully, and yet somehow I'm still unhappy."

But the assumptions of the Covenant create a mesmerizing mirage, a collective illusion, from beginning to end. If you really start to question any of the Covenant's underlying assumptions, its empty illusion is quickly revealed. Why must all women be super-model-thin and seek to emulate standards best evoked by a Barbie doll? Will dieting actually make us thin over the long run? And hey—wait just a minute—why are we all dying to be so thin anyhow? Because it will make us happy? Because "thinness equals happiness" is some kind of eternal formula for living happily ever after?

If that's true, then impoverished women who don't have enough to eat must be very happy, because they're very thin. This statement is offensive and ridiculous. But it's also offensive that as women in the overly abundant Western world, we give our lives to the empty illusion of starving for happiness, while women in less fortunate parts of the world might well believe that having more to eat could certainly bring them some happiness.

Seeing our Western obsession with food and thinness in the

context of our planet as a whole helps us to see how ridiculous and pointless it is. There's obviously more to life than our empty and meaningless pursuit of thinness.

seeing through the illusion

The Covenant must also no longer be working for you, or you wouldn't be reading this book. Maybe the last magic weight-loss formula you tried was effective for a while, then stopped working. Now you're trying to figure out how to make it work again. Or maybe you're just tired of the whole thing and looking for a new way out. Whether we know it or not, when we buy into the Covenant and equate happiness with thinness, we are in fact trapped. The links that make up the chains of the trap are quite deceptive. To many of us, they look like the very elements we think will bring us freedom. If you look closely, you might see a chain that's composed of measuring spoons, scales, calorie charts, exercise regimes, lists of food dos and don'ts, rights and wrongs, and all of the other external behaviors that we've been taught will help us to stay thin and happy.

In this chapter we'll examine the tiny links that make up the chain. They are the endless little moments—trains of thought and modes of behavior—that form habits that keep you stuck.

Any one of these moments may seem harmless in and of itself. So what if you're conscientious and weigh your food portions? What's the problem with not eating any carbohydrates at breakfast and lunch? How can it hurt you to stick to your exercise schedule no matter what? In isolation, any of these behaviors might not only seem harmless, it might in fact be considered intelligent and well chosen. That is, if you're conscious that you're choosing them at all. The most insidious links in the chain are those that became habits so long ago that we haven't been consciously aware of them for years.

We can achieve real, lasting change by bringing mindfulness to our unconscious food habits. Mindfulness helps us to see that the dieting game is just that: an illusion, at best. It has nothing to do with real, lasting happiness.

When you know what *you* want in life, and what's at stake if you forfeit real meaning, your perspective begins to shift. You start to reassess and question everything, holding your patterns of behavior up to the light of consciousness. By examining your current behaviors and observing your patterns, you can learn how to repattern, making choices that are in line with your overall intention for life.

the essence of food

Throughout this book, we've been examining *your* essence—your dharma, or personal purpose. Every person has a unique purpose, the character that defines their personal essence.

Eastern philosophy takes this belief in individual nature one step further by recognizing that *everything* has an essence—a unique character—that makes it one thing and not another. In the Indian tradition this principle is called *rasa*. Rasa is the unchanging element at the center of any form of life.

The concept of rasa is rich, with a multitude of meanings on many levels. On its most outward level, rasa means "taste." More subtly, rasa is defined as the juice of any object, its marrow or sap. On the esoteric level, rasa is thought of as the essence of any object, that which is the best, finest, or prime part of an entity. With food, as with all living beings, rasa is the quality that defines and identifies the ultimate nature.

Rasa is also used to describe how things are shaped by the unique circumstances of their existence. An apple, for instance, has its defining characteristics of apple-ness: its shape, skin, flesh, sweetness, and juiciness. But each individual apple is also different from the next, due to circumstantial factors such as weather, its position on the tree, and when it was picked.

146

deepening your food practice

By cultivating your ability to perceive the rasa of foods, you can discover your own balanced, individual path to eating. But in our everyday eating experience, we all too often stop at the outermost layer of naming the familiar taste of a food—sweet is chocolate cake, salty is a potato chip, pungent is garlic. If we're to find the real rasa in the foods we eat, we must start at the surface level of tastes and textures and move down to the quintessence.

If we stop at the surface level of food, we reduce it to a concept that's so well known to us that we can dismiss it. We become unconscious, and the eating experience is transformed into a quick mental sound bite: "I know that taste, that's the sweetness of a chocolate cake." We chew mechanically, unaware of the greater depths of rasa that particular food has to offer us on this particular day.

When we apprehend the rasa of a food, we experience the intricacies of the essence of sweetness, or the nature of astringent, or the ultimate being of pungent. In this way we can personally, intimately connect with the juice, the marrow, the prime reality, of any food as it is in the present moment.

Food practices can help us open up to the experiences of tasting the rasa. This means tasting the individual characteristics of the foods you eat, as well as learning how to remain conscious and present throughout the whole eating experience.

PRACTICE: TASTING THE RASA

We're all experts on the foods we love and hate. We know exactly what licorice is, what to expect from a glass of tart lemonade, and just how long it takes to scarf down a candy bar. But how often do we really savor the essence of the food that's set before us?

By tuning into your own feedback, and the interplay of all of your individual senses, you can hone in on a food's essence so that you experience it fully.

1. Set aside about twenty minutes when you won't be interrupted. Make sure to start the practice at a point in your day when you're hungry but not famished.

2. Select three of your favorite foods. If possible, choose foods that require no preparation and can be eaten with your hands (a piece of fruit, some cheese, or a cookie, for example). Place the foods on a table in front of you. Close your eyes and take a moment to clear your mind.

3. Open your eyes and look carefully at the foods, examining each one fully, taking in its visual appearance. Then make a choice: pick one of the three foods as the one you'll eat, and reach for it.

4. The instant your fingers touch the food, broaden your awareness to include your sense of touch. Pay attention to

the physical sensation of the food against your fingers: its texture, firmness, temperature, and so on.

5. Now bring the food close to your mouth and prepare to take a bite. You may detect a shift in temperature around your lips as you bring the food close to your mouth. Engage your sense of smell, paying attention to the most subtle of aromas. Note also that what you smell may be influenced by the temperature or moisture of the food, or it may be mixed with other smells from your environment.

6. Take a bite of the food. Notice the variety of sounds associated with biting into the food. Are the sounds that you hear crunchy, soft, rhythmic, slurping, sucking, wet, or dry? Notice that all of this happens—the visual, tactile, olfactory, and aural sensing—before you've even tasted the food.

7. Now engage your sense of taste. Are the flavors sour, sweet, spicy, pungent, or aromatic? Do you taste more than one flavor at once, or does one taste dominate, then another come forth?

Reflection: This food practice demonstrates that learning to taste and appreciate a food's rasa is a complex art. It gives us insight into how our physical senses work. We may ordinarily jump to the conclusion that we like or dislike something because of its taste. But this practice shows that a food appeals or doesn't based on all five senses. The practice also establishes a format for becoming more conscious as we eat.

savoring rasa

What you'll find is that if you make the effort to tune into the rasa of food, you'll find it more and more difficult to eat mindlessly—to graze, pig out, go into a food coma, or any other unconscious mode of eating. When you savor the intricacies of food, the eating experience becomes increasingly vivid.

The juiciness of a peach, for instance, actually consists of a complex blend of composite parts: wateriness, viscosity, sweetness, and tartness, all of which contribute to its "peachiness." You'll also begin to notice that the flavors and qualities of foods have a component of timing—some flavors burst forth in your first bite of food, other flavors begin later, and some linger on after the initial taste disappears.

By fine-tuning how you perceive the intricacies of what you're eating, you experience subtle levels of a food's essence. Through this increased awareness, you'll begin to recognize what it is about a food that deeply appeals to you. When you feel the call of hunger, you'll be able to judge whether a particular food is the optimal choice for attaining balanced satisfaction.

You can use the above exercise to truly experience a food's rasa, helping you to break destructive food habits. For example, if you eat your favorite candy bar with the intention of staying conscious and tuning into its rasa, your awakened experience of the food might surprise you. You might discover that the candy's highly refined sugars, hydrogenated oils, artificial colors and flavors—not to mention a whole host of preservatives with hard-to-pronounce names—don't seem so seductive after all. By observing rasa and your feedback, you might eventually find for yourself that a beautiful, juicy, ripe apple in season provides more joy and contentment than the most "sinful" food from your most wicked food fantasies.

The part of you that's awake and brimming with life, and therefore vulnerable when exposed, may begin to feel assaulted by foods you once loved: extremely spicy foods, or those that contain highly refined ingredients, artificial ingredients, chemicals, and preservatives. On the other hand, a once seemingly boring piece of fruit may become far more interesting and appealing than you ever imagined.

practical practices for daily life

Now it's time to take our search for essence into the trenches of our everyday lives. What's most nurturing for any one of us to eat is a highly individual matter. Some people seem to do best eating a higher proportion of protein, while others thrive on a diet high in carbohydrates. Some need small amounts of food often through-out the day, while others do well eating three bigger meals and no snacks. Vegetarianism makes some people feel energetic and vi-brant, while others feel weak or become run-down without meat in their diet.

To complicate matters further, what was perfectly balanced and nourishing for us at one point in our lives may be precisely the wrong food for us to eat in another phase. That's why tuning into food on the deepest level—through its rasa—is essential. When you're conscious of how the rasa of a food interacts with your own rasa, you can judge what's right for you at any point in time. If we're going to escape our old dieting mentality once and for all, we must learn to trust our ability to find balance in the foods we eat.

But actualizing this practice in the real world can be a chal-lenge. In everyday life, you're constantly faced with choices that can free you or keep you stuck. Many of us opt out of consciously making our own choices when we follow a set diet that makes the choices for us.

Letting go of the safety net that diets provide, having to trust your own instincts, can seem terrifying. If you've depended for years on one formula or another, you may wonder, "If I don't fol-low a diet, then what *do* I do?" You may feel that, stripped of dieting rules, you're standing at the edge of a cliff, ready to fall into a menacing abyss.

The following "Practical Practices" can serve as your training wheels. With practical planning, you'll be able to see the strength and direction within yourself to find your own path to balance.

Your mission now is to learn to recognize from the inside out exactly what, when, and how much you need to eat to satisfy yourself and be happy. As you learn to appreciate the essence of foods you eat, and how to apply consciousness to all aspects of your life, you'll begin to trust yourself.

PRACTICAL PRACTICE: SAYING GRACE

One very effective way to stay conscious and full of intention while you eat is the age-old custom of saying grace before a meal. An expression of gratitude for food has been customary in most cultures throughout history. Saying grace helps us to recognize how lucky we are to have the food we're about to eat, and to feel thankful for its sustenance. Grace acknowledges that having enough to eat isn't to be taken for granted. It's also an opportunity to experience your place in the life cycle, to recognize that both you and the food you eat are forms of life, parts of a greater whole.

Saying grace need not have religious connotations. Rather, it's an opportunity to bring your deepest sense of meaning to the act of eating. Without food, you'll die, and to live a meaningful existence, you need both food and purpose. Saying grace affirms both of these greater truths. It helps you actively set your intention to stay mindful and fully conscious as you eat.

1. Start by taking a moment to clear your mind. With your eyes closed, notice any physical sensations, emotions, and thoughts you're experiencing.

2. Next, open your eyes and take in the food visually. Try to be aware of its qualities and presence. Acknowledge its life—the life you'll now consume so that you can go on living. Try to tap into your sense of gratitude, whatever this means to you personally.

3. If there's a particular prayer, chant, or phrase that you like to observe before a meal, use that. If you don't have a grace you know or like, you can create your own. The expression need only be a sincere indication of your thanks.

4. Now say out loud the grace you've chosen. If speaking out loud feels uncomfortable, you may say grace silently. Eventually, saying it aloud may bring more intensity to the experience for you. When you finish, take another moment to appreciate the connection between you and the

food you're about to eat. Then begin eating and enjoy the meal.

Reflection: Saying grace helps us to bring our sense of personal purpose, and an awareness of the bigger picture of life, to the forefront of our minds as we sit down to eat. It also helps us to be more conscious and aware of the actual act of eating as we infuse it with meaning. When we take time to say grace before a meal, eating can become an exercise of meaning.

PRACTICAL PRACTICE: FLEXIBLE PLANNING

Planning can be both a boon and a bane for making the switch from formulaic eating to a more intuitive approach. On one hand, planning is essential. It allows you to check in with what you want to eat, helps you to make sure that you have the foods you need on hand, and gives you an opportunity to design a balanced approach to food that feels right for *you.*

On the other hand, planning can be problematic if you become too rigid, sticking to a plan whether or not it feels appropriate when it's time to eat. You also might find yourself using the plan as just another diet that takes you away from your own feedback.

A natural by-product of any structured plan is the alluring possibility of cheating. For example, if you follow a diet that includes a cheating loophole, the fantasy is that you can have your cake, eat it too, and *still* lose ten pounds a week! The game we play with ourselves is that you can "cheat" if you make up for it later.

Cheating typically begins as an attempt to balance the out-of-control urges brought on by deprivation. But underlying this method of "planning" is the belief that your desires and feedback must be ignored.

The secret of planning, then, is to give up the game both of cheating and of playing by the rules. Planning is the art of using your inner sensibilities to find harmony. Both your eating blueprint, and what you actually eat, must be based on your own internal indicators of health and well-being. The following suggestions can help you begin to find that balance.

deciding what and when to eat: You may find it effective to plan all of your meals a week ahead of time. Or you may prefer to plan your meals for just one day. Having a clear idea about what you'll be eating at your next meal is very helpful.

Planning lets you know what lies ahead, rather than facing a limitless unknown. If you have a plan at meal- or snack-time, you're less likely to make haphazard choices.

Planning also makes grocery shopping much less of a crapshoot. Shopping can be a chore that presents a series of stress-inducing temptations. You may find yourself avoiding certain aisles in the grocery store because they contain foods that are so "dangerous" you don't even want to get near them in case they'll leap off the shelves and into your cart. But with a planned menu and the items you'll need on a list, you're less likely to wind up tossing all sorts of extraneous items into the cart.

Finally, planning is a great time-saver when it comes to cooking. For example, you can clean more than one meal's worth of salad greens or vegetables at a time. Or you can cook up twice the rice you'll need for one meal, knowing you'll use the leftovers in a different dish a couple of days later.

Knowing what you'll be cooking also helps you figure out how much time you'll need to prepare your meals. That way you're less likely to find yourself famished shortly before dinnertime, with an hour's worth of cooking to do before you can eat.

Stay in touch with your feedback throughout the planning process. Pay attention to your gut feelings about what you want to eat. Sometimes you may not feel at all like eating what you'd planned. It's important not to stick to the plan just because it's the plan. By listening to your feedback, you'll know what your body wants and needs.

planning a balanced meal: Another aspect of planning is constructing balanced meals. The question, of course, is "What is a balanced meal?" The simple answer is that a balanced meal is one that fosters good health. Complexities arise immediately with this statement. How do you know whether a food is helping or hindering your health?

Some experts say a protein-rich diet will make you healthy; others insist that one high in carbohydrates will do the trick. Other methods propound that your blood type, your activity level, or even your complexion are how you should determine your diet.

There are countless systematized and external ways of judging what we should or shouldn't eat. The confusing part is that virtually every diet has at least a seed of truth to it. For example, protein *is* good for you. But that doesn't necessarily mean that eating a high-protein diet is the answer for everyone. Following almost any diet will initially make you feel better after a period of eating in an unconscious and off-balance way. When you start to pay more attention to what you eat, and adjust the balance of your foods, you experience beneficial physical changes—for a while.

When you feel better, you might believe that this diet indeed offers *the* magical solution. But when your new eating program inevitably slips back into yet another mindless routine, you find yourself once again looking for a new solution.

The problem with any diet is when we eat without mindfulness. The key to finding a balanced diet is staying mindful and tuning into your feedback. Follow these basic guidelines to sculpt your own personalized balanced diet.

First, eat whole foods that are as unprocessed as possible. This means fresh foods, preferably organic (those that are grown without the use of artificial chemicals, pesticides, and herbicides). It's essential to read labels carefully to know exactly what you're eating. Try to limit prepackaged foods and those that contain artificial ingredients and preservatives.

Creating balance means including some protein, some carbohydrate, and a small amount of fat at every meal. How you balance these three depends on your system on any given day. This also implies that you know what foods are good sources of protein, carbohydrate, and fat.

When considering balance, include beverages in your planning. It's vital to drink plenty of water every day.

To quickly evaluate a meal for balance, ask yourself the following questions:

1. Is there at least one source each of protein, carbohydrate, and fat in the meal?
2. Does the plate look appealing, with a balance of colors and shapes? (Having foods of various colors usually ensures a wider range of nutrients.)

3. Do the textures of the foods blend and complement one another?

4. Do the spices and aromas enhance rather than compete with
one another?

When you're eating foods that are balanced for your constitution, you know it. You don't feel overly full, yet you're not hungry;
you don't feel sluggish or jittery. Instead, you have a consistent energy to carry you through the day. You sleep well, have good diges-
tion, and your skin and hair are healthy-looking. You don't usually
have headaches, a runny nose, or fatigue. When you're eating a balanced diet, you simply feel healthy.

Of course, many other factors contribute to this overall feeling
of balance, including sleep, exercise, and the mindfulness you bring
to the rest of your life. But your diet is critical in determining your
health.

who plans to cook?: Perhaps the biggest stumbling block to eating
healthy foods is that someone has to prepare them. With the pace
of modern life, cooking the way our grandmothers did—for hours
a day, making bread and all sorts of other goodies from scratch—is
less and less realistic. For many, it's not even desirable. Since cooking takes up so much of your time, why bother when what you

want is as close as your phone? Reasonably priced foods are so readily available—at delis, supermarkets, and from carryout menus—that often it may seem just as practical and cost-effective to order out as it is to cook.

But one big concern when you don't prepare your own meals is that you can *never* be certain exactly what goes into them. When you cook for yourself, you know the quality and the rasa of the ingredients that you're preparing. You can really start to get a feeling for the taste of a fresh, ripe tomato, or the capacity of a rice kernel to burst forth and transform as it's cooked.

When you cook what you eat, and bring your conscious awareness to the act of cooking, you experience the food more fully. When you cook with intention and consciousness, the food comes to life in your hands. You mold the ingredients, work them, encourage or temper them. You learn to enhance their flavor and are delighted by the aromas and textures they give back as you prepare them.

To make cooking a pleasurable part of how you relate to food, follow these basic planning guidelines.

1. Allow yourself ample time to cook so that you don't feel rushed just before you eat.
2. Make recipes in stages. Check recipes for steps that can be

what are you hungry for?

done hours or even days in advance, such as mixing ingredients for a quick bread, marinating a dish, or trimming and cleaning all the vegetables for a stir-fry.

3. Be sure to have all the ingredients on hand when you begin cooking. Arrange them on the countertop so that you can focus on the process of cooking, rather than wasting time searching for what you need.

4. Have the basic tools and equipment ready. It helps to have your kitchen well organized so you can easily find the right tools.

5. Clean up as you cook. Washing a few dishes or tidying up the counter between steps can spare you an overwhelming mess to clean up at the end.

including exercise as part of the plan: Just as you must eat, sleep, and stimulate your mind each day, you should also incorporate exercise on a daily basis. Here we're referring to some form of aerobic exercise that gets your blood moving, your muscles engaged, and your heart pumping. You may like to walk, bicycle, run, play a sport, or work out at the gym. There are endless possibilities for exercising; the only challenge is finding—or planning—the time. As with planning your food, you need to schedule exercise into your day.

As part of your search for balance, you must jettison the "no pain, no gain" mentality that's so prevalent in our society. It's far better to find an activity that you really enjoy, so that you can eradicate the "exercise *is* a pain" mentality. Just as conscious eating is part of what keeps us balanced, so is mindful attention to how, when, and how much we exercise. When you exercise with mindfulness, your overall intention is to bring balance and well-being to your system.

what are you eating right now?

On any given day, at any given moment, you have the potential to create a completely new relationship to eating. The secret formula for making radical change is very simple: if you can become more and more mindful as you eat, you'll most certainly change what you eat and bring yourself naturally into balance.

These words are easy to say. Learning how to actually make them work is what the practices in this book are designed to do. If only it were as easy as saying, "Oh, yeah, that makes sense, from here on out I'll be more conscious and I'll have no more problems!"

But as you've experienced in the food practices and in your mind/body practices, being present is very difficult. At first you might find that you can maintain only the tiniest bit of conscious-ness. The whole effort hardly seems worth it. But if you stick with the practices, they can and will change your life. You won't change what you eat because you have to, or because it's right or wrong by anyone else's standards. Change will start to take place quite natu-rally. Because you care so much about becoming more aligned with your own internal sense of balance, it will feel good just to be guided by your gut instinct. You'll want to become more and more conscious because it feels so good to wake up to what you need on the deepest level.

That's why these food practices have nothing to do with willpower or deprivation. They have everything to do with acting out of your own profound motivation for fulfillment. Being con-scious means that we're responsible for dealing with who we cur-rently are and what we currently need.

Learning how to change your relationship to food and your body can take time. In our fast-food culture, we want salvation right now, or at the latest by tomorrow morning. But if you're a veteran of all of the latest greatest diets, you know that "fast" and "lasting" don't usually come together. To achieve change that lasts into the future, you have to begin right now.

So tomorrow morning, when you wake up, your body will look more or less the same, your clothes will fit the same, and you'll be dealing with the same surrounding culture and world. But the difference will be inside of you—you'll no longer be seeing through the eyes of illusion. You'll be seeing things just as they are right now. And you'll keep on doing that: seeing things as they are at any given moment.

When you're no longer blind to your own habits and behaviors, when you wake up to the vibrancy of the foods that you eat and the life that you're living, the change has already come. You're discovering reliable and penetrating tools that will help you to always know what you're really hungry for.

NINE

the conscious choice

Any girl can be glamorous. All you have to do is stand still and look stupid.

—HEDY LAMARR, ACTRESS (ONCE BILLED AS THE
"WORLD'S MOST BEAUTIFUL WOMAN")

pretty as a picture

All women are impossibly thin, eternally young, and preternat-
urally beautiful. At least that's what you'd believe if you got your
idea of what women look like from magazines, movies, or TV.

When we see these images of the unattainably ideal female, we get the message loud and clear: "Beauty at any cost."

Not to worry—if you're not naturally endowed with super-model beauty, then our modern society offers many options for faking it: nose jobs, breast enlargements, tummy tucks, tanning booths, wrinkle-prevention cream, and everybody's favorite, starvation.

Buried deep in our hearts may be the echo of knowledge that beauty is only skin-deep, but we still believe that we must somehow meet our culture's standards of beauty. Like Cinderella's wicked stepsisters who tried in vain to stuff their oversize feet into the tiny glass slipper, we find ourselves molding our bodies to fit a contrived notion of how we should look.

As women, we're faced with a particular paradox. How do we feel beautiful just the way we are and still try to model ourselves after those elusive standards? From the time we're very small, we're indoctrinated by phrases such as "Pretty as a picture" and "It takes pain to be beautiful." We internalize the mantra "Beauty at any cost."

On rare days, we manage to coordinate what we consider to be an acceptable presentation of our hair, complexion, and weight. For just a moment, we're almost in reach of "winning" the beauty game. But even at that split instant when we're closest to having it all together, we may realize that there's still something missing. When does our own inner beauty, the truth of who we are, enter into the picture? Eventually we may begin to wonder what beauty really is, and what we're chasing.

The vision of great beauty has forever haunted and eluded humanity. The siren song of beauty draws us but remains always barely beyond our all-too-grasping human reach. Like so many of our finest illusions, just as we think we understand beauty, have it, can hold on to it, it slips away. Why?

It's because beauty isn't an idea or a standard, it's a state of being. Beauty *is* in the eye of the beholder. What makes a person, words, flowers, or a plate of food beautiful is an individual reaction that can't be quantified. Beauty reveals itself in the flash of a moment as we perceive any object or concept as beautiful. Why any one of us finds something attractive or repulsive, beautiful or ugly, delicious or disgusting has to do with our own personal aesthetic, our personal sense of taste. The word "aesthetic" is defined as "being appreciative or responsible to the beautiful." To understand our own sense of aesthetic, understanding how we perceive beauty (particularly our own) is essential for women. An aesthetic sense is completely personal, something that we develop and nurture within ourselves. We must learn to explore and trust how beauty feels to *us*. We can then evolve a sense of our own inner aesthetic and develop a personal expression of beauty that reflects who we really are.

For women with a food and body conflict, expressing beauty can get very convoluted. We swing back and forth between extremes. We either do our level best to win the beauty game by any mortifications of the flesh we deem necessary, or we let our looks "go to hell" as we resist feminine entrapment in a patriarchal society.

Fighting your genuine desire to be attractive is no more satisfying than attempting to model your appearance on external standards. The desire to look your best is natural and healthy. What's essential is to learn how to determine for yourself what *you* find aesthetically pleasing. By nurturing and asserting your own internal standard of beauty, you can honestly express the beauty of who you *are,* not who you wish you *were.*

developing your own food aesthetic

We also need to assert our own aesthetic when it comes to choosing the foods we eat. Our aesthetic determines the foods that we're attracted to, and those that repulse us. With food, this sense of aesthetic goes far beyond the flavors. Our food aesthetic is based on all of our senses, as well as our mental and emotional impressions.

Before we even take our first bite, we may find ourselves strongly drawn to this "delicacy," or revolted by that "junk."

But when we're actively in touch with our aesthetic sensibilities, this attraction or repulsion comes from our own internal connection to the innate quality—the rasa—of the food. In this sense, aesthetic is something much more than mere preference or taste. The Indian sage Abhinavagupta proposed that aesthetic was an inborn quality that bursts forth within us, like a seed that lies dormant until it encounters truth or beauty and springs to life.

This bursting is the internal feeling that lets us know we're in the presence of true beauty. It happens when our gut sensibility resonates with rasa. It's a source of great pleasure. It can happen as we bite into a perfectly ripe apple, see a beautiful painting, listen to music, or look at nature.

However, that blissful moment is only one aspect of the aesthetic experience. Equally important is the function our aesthetic serves in helping us to critically evaluate what foods are right or wrong for us at any given moment. Our aesthetic allows us to weigh all of our impressions of a food (its visual appearance, how we feel about it, our intellectual assessment of it) against our gut sensibility so that we can use our critical faculties to choose the right foods.

But when we lose or ignore the connection to our aesthetic, food can't satisfy us deeply. We may feed ourselves until we're physically full, even stuffed. Or we may deprive ourselves of food, trying to mold our bodies to some external notion of beauty. Without that connection to our aesthetic, we're literally starving for beauty in either case.

For most of us, aesthetic isn't at the top of our minds under ordinary circumstances, particularly when we're eating. At best we might notice an attractive arrangement of food on a plate, or the pleasant ambience of a restaurant. But normally we're so busy counting calories and fat grams, fearing the cheesecake or embracing the celery stick, that we lose our aesthetic connection altogether. Being directed by unconscious habits, losing our active connection to the rasa of the food, is the opposite of the aesthetic experience.

If we start to look more closely, we can discover the details that make up the aesthetic experience of any meal: the comfort of the environment; the tastes, aromas, visual presentation of the food; how we're feeling; the company we're with. When we connect with our aesthetic, the meal comes to life and satisfies us on a much deeper level. Using your aesthetic sensibility to make the right choices for *you* is the actual "magic formula" you've been looking for all of these years. You simply need to learn how to invoke it, and to apply your aesthetic when evaluating what and when to eat.

PRACTICE: LOOKING ANEW

Compare how differently you approach foods that you eat often with foods that you've never eaten. When you're eating familiar foods, or those that you have a set idea about—"gourmet, fattening, dietetic, sinful"—you tend to eat out of habit. Because you think you know that food, you miss out on its rasa. But when you eat a new food, you have fewer preconceived notions about it. You're open to how it measures up against your inner food aesthetic.

The following exercise helps you identify ways in which you habitually relate to food, and enables you to discover your own aesthetic.

1. Set aside about twenty minutes during which you won't be interrupted. Make sure to start the practice at a point in your day when you're hungry but not famished.
2. Select two foods: one that you've never eaten before and another that you eat often. Prepare small portions of each food, at most three or four mouthfuls.
3. Place the familiar food in front of you. Close your eyes and take a moment to clear your mind.
4. Now open your eyes and look at the food without touching it. In your journal, write a few statements describing how

you perceive the food. Also detail how you're reacting to the food physically, emotionally, and mentally. For example, are you attracted to what you see or smell? Is your mouth watering? What expectations do you have about eating the food?

5. Now pick up the food and eat it. When you're finished, make note of how attentive you were to the entire process of eating. Did your sensations, thoughts, and feelings match your expectations? How did the tastes and other physical sensations of eating change from the first bite to the last? What did you notice about the food itself that was different from what you'd anticipated?

6. Take several moments to clear your palate. It might be helpful to drink some water, or to stand up and stretch, before continuing with the exercise.

7. When you're ready, place the food you've never eaten in front of you. Close your eyes and take a moment to clear your mind.

8. Now open your eyes and look closely at the food without touching it. What initially strikes you about the food? What do you see or smell that draws you to it or puts you off? What are your thoughts or expectations about this food?

9. Write about how you're perceiving the food as you prepare to eat it—what you see and smell, as well as your mental and

emotional states. Are you curious about some aspect of the food, anticipating a particular experience of taste, tentative about the idea of eating the food?

10. Now pick up the food. As you take your first bite, concentrate on the many subtle aspects of the eating experience. Focus on what the food feels like as you pick it up, what you're thinking and feeling as you bring the food close to your mouth. Notice how much food you eat with your first bite—a daring mouthful or just a nibble. Where do you place the food inside your mouth as your tongue explores the tastes for the first time? Slow down the process of experiencing the food so that you can track your feelings and perceptions carefully.

11. Now take a second bite. Have your attitudes and perceptions altered in any way since your first bite? Are the tastes, aromas, and textures as strong as they were originally? Notice your physical, emotional, and mental reactions to the food.

Reflection: This exercise helps you break free of unconscious eating habits. In the future, when you notice yourself contemplating a food habitually, or eating without mindfulness, you can recall what it's like to eat a food for the first time. Remember how it feels to have no expectations about a food and allow yourself to fully experience the food's rasa.

When we eat new foods, we typically have more questions than answers. Because we don't know what to expect, we're open to discovering whether or not we find a food aesthetically pleasing.

You can approach familiar foods in this same way, suspending your expectations by engaging your mindfulness. In reality, your experience of any food is never the same twice. Even a food you think you're completely familiar with, like your favorite kosher dill, varies from pickle to pickle. How you savor that pickle will also depend on what's going on as you're eating—your emotions, thoughts, and physical sensations of the moment. But you can experience these subtle differences in a familiar food, and fully engage your aesthetic, only when you're paying attention.

the call of hunger

As human beings, we're susceptible to cravings for a great many things that can lead to addictive or troubled behavior, including drugs, alcohol, and lust for power. The desire for food can cause comparable cravings and destructive behaviors, but the difference is that food is something we can't live without.

what are you hungry for?

Hunger is a primal response to a lack of food. Until we eat, our body gives us increasingly strong signals telling us that we're hungry. But women with a food and body conflict often don't know what it feels like to be truly hungry.

We don't eat when we're hungry because we fear our voracious appetite will put on the pounds. Or we eat when we're not hungry because we're bored, depressed, or anxious. When we eat in these habitual ways, we obscure the ability to recognize whether or not we're truly hungry. We don't trust ourselves to gauge our own hunger.

Because hunger is such a primary urge, it can't be ignored for long. We may deny it, refuse to give into it, or wire our jaw shut for a virtuoso show of willpower. But hunger still affects us on the most fundamental levels. It makes us weak, off balance, unclear, and full of pain. Although we may be able to defer eating as long as possible, hunger will take its toll over the long haul of our lives.

Somewhere between starving for slimness and overeating for comfort is the capacity to recognize your true hunger.

your body's hunger

So, how do you know you're hungry? Is it when your stomach grumbles or your mouth waters at the thought of a pizza? Or is it because it's dinnertime and there's an alluring smell of onions frying in a pan? Is it because it's five-thirty P.M. and you always eat at five-thirty P.M.? Or did you just have a fight with your husband and suddenly you're starving for french fries?

It can be hard to recognize hunger. Its physical symptoms can be subtle. We might feel tired, a tightness in the jaw, or a mild headache, but it may not occur to us that these are hunger signals. From a young age, we're taught to suppress hunger. As children, we must eat at a designated mealtime, not when we're hungry. We're warned that if we snack, we'll "ruin our appetites." In fact, that's what we end up doing—we learn how to eat in a regimented ways, rather than according to our true appetite: our hunger.

Emotions can also make it difficult to know when we're hungry. Stress, sadness, or fear can produce physical sensations that are almost identical to our body's true hunger signals. For example, tightness in the throat can indicate either emotional stress or physical hunger. "Butterflies" in the abdomen feel similar to a grumbling, hungry stomach. These emotional states can cause us to eat when we don't need food. When we confuse physical and emotional hunger, eating can become a destructive habit.

Physical signs of hunger can also be confounded when we superimpose associations and memories on to food. We might associate the love of our grandmother with the comforting smell of chicken soup. Or maybe we remember how romantically happy we were in Paris when we ate a croissant. Now, when we eat these foods, we imbue them with the hope of bringing back a happy memory.

For all of these reasons, knowing when we're hungry can be a very challenging task. But until we can accurately recognize our body's signs of hunger and respond appropriately, we can't resolve a food and body conflict.

PRACTICE: CONSCIOUS STRATEGIES—HUNGER

The following strategies can help you learn how to trust your instincts and know when you're hungry. Rather than feeling you must rely on a diet or any other formula, rely on feedback and mindfulness to tell you how to satisfy your hunger.

strategy 1: learn to differentiate between hunger, habits, and urges: When you get a feeling of hunger, the most important thing you can do is to acknowledge it. Simply note, "I feel hungry." When we're not consciously paying attention to a hunger signal, we may eat automatically as soon as our stomach grumbles. Or we may try to ignore our hunger signals and shove them away. Don't jump to any conclusions about your hunger—just be aware of it.

A hunger signal may in fact mean you're hungry. But it could also mean a dozen other things—you're bored, you're sad, you need some motivation to get working, or it's noon and you always eat at noon. Generally, we can separate the signals that prompt us to eat into three categories: hunger, urges, or habits. Feedback can help you differentiate between these.

After you get a hunger signal, allow yourself to concentrate on the feeling. Listen to what your feedback is saying to you. Close your eyes if it helps you to focus on all of the feedback that accompanies the message telling you to eat. Is your feedback telling you that you want Chee•tos since you always eat them as you drive to work? Or is the hunger message saying "Cookie" like a flashing red sign? Or are you feeling dizzy, and you realize it's been seven hours since you ate anything? If you determine that the message telling you to eat isn't true physical hunger, then it's an urge or a habit. Read on to the next practice, "Conscious Strategies: Habits and Urges" (see page 191), where we'll address how to deal with urges and habits.

To determine your own physical signs of true hunger, you need to listen to your feedback over time. You may notice a variety of physical symptoms that indicate hunger—one day a dryness in the throat, another day a feeling of dizziness. But no matter what the particular symptom, you will always feel a clear indication that you need food every time you're hungry. You can rely on that. Eventually, your very own unique message of "I'm hungry" becomes unmistakable. When you hear that message, you'll know that you really *are* hungry. Knowing the difference between true hunger and urges or habits can derail unconscious eating behaviors before you get carried away by them.

strategy 2: figure out what you're hungry for: Once you've determined you're genuinely hungry, it's time to consider what food will satisfy you. Start by closing your eyes and tapping into your hunger. Ask yourself: "What food am I hungry for?" You may just get an abstract feeling about the kind of food you want to eat—something creamy, salty, soothing, aromatic. Or you may picture exactly what you'd like to eat—a banana, some pretzels, or lasagna.

If you get an abstract feeling, engage your senses and picture some different foods that might satisfy the feeling. If nothing comes to mind immediately, keep trying so that the food you choose will be the right one.

Then take the next step and imagine eating the food. Does it seem as though the food will actually satisfy you? Or did the food initially sound good, like the thought of lasagna, but then you're struck by the feeling that the mound of cheese and noodles will be too heavy? If that's the case, close your eyes again and keep trying to identify the right food to satisfy your hunger.

You might feel a sense of conflict if the food you think you're hungry for is "unhealthy" or "fattening." You may also feel conflicted if you try to insist to yourself that what you really *should* be hungry for is something "healthy" and "low-calorie." In both cases, you're ignoring what you're really hungry for. When you don't eat what your body is telling you it needs, your hunger doesn't get satisfied.

But you *will* feel satisfied when you eat according to your intuition. And simultaneously, you'll find the right balance of food for your body. You may fear that if you eat intuitively, you'll gorge wildly and gain a million pounds. But by using mindfulness and these conscious eating strategies, you can stop playing unconscious eating games. When you're conscious and filled with a sense of purpose, you'll learn how to eat the right foods to satisfy your hunger. You'll simply feel content.

strategy 3: you don't have to be in the clean-plate club: Once you've decided what to eat, listen to your feedback to determine the quantity of food that will satisfy you. Do you want just a snack, or do you need a meal? Do you need a small meal, or are you very hungry and in need of a good-sized meal?

Many of us are in the habit of eating whatever is on our plate just because it's there. We were told as children, "Think of all the people who are starving in other parts of the world." At the time it may have occurred to us that eating more food than we wanted wasn't really helpful to those less fortunate. But as we obediently tried to clean the plate, we acquired yet another unconscious behavior.

For many of us, our mealtime goal remains to empty the plate, regardless of our hunger. If we're at a restaurant and we get a plate brimming over with more food than three people can eat, we try to eat it all because it's there. At an all-you-can-eat buffet, the sky's the limit—we can fill the plate endlessly. At home, we eat until the plate is empty; that's how we know we're full.

But your only accurate measure of hunger comes from within you, not from an arbitrarily sized plate. Any measured portion of food—a plate, a bag, a serving size—can't be relied on to tell you how much you need to eat. Only *you* know how hungry you are, and how much you need to eat to feel satisfied. Before you begin eating, set your intention: to stop eating when you've had enough. Then, as you eat, pause periodically to check in with your feedback and ask yourself: "Do I feel physically satisfied?"

No matter how much food you have in front of you, pledge to eat only as much as you need to feel satisfied. That may mean eating only half of what's on your plate. Or it may mean breaking the taboo and, like Oliver, asking for more. Eat the right amount now, feel satisfied, and avoid mindlessly stuffing yourself later.

strategy 4: learn how to know when enough is enough: The key to knowing when you've had enough food is to actively pay attention to how your hunger changes as you eat. If you're talking, reading a newspaper, or watching TV while you eat, you're not paying conscious attention to your hunger. You may not stop eating until you suddenly get the feeling "Whoa! I'm stuffed out of my gourd! I'm going to explode!"

How did you go from being hungry to having eaten way too much? The missing link is your consciousness. When you eat mindlessly, it's as if you have a very insensitive gas gauge that doesn't rise as you pour in the fuel. The gauge starts out at empty, then suddenly makes a huge leap to way past the full mark.

This happens because somewhere in between the first and last bites of food, you become unconscious. You eat multiple bites of food and swallow each and every one of them quite willingly, not paying attention to your signs of bodily hunger. As a result, your gauge goes to full, and you're stuffed.

The best strategy to counter a faulty gauge is to slow down your eating. Stop frequently throughout your meal, putting down your utensil for just an instant. Then close your eyes and check your fullness level by tuning into your feedback. Ask yourself the question "If I stop eating right now, am I satisfied, or will I still be hungry?" If you feel genuinely satisfied, stop, even if you've eaten much less than you usually do. And if you still feel hungry, keep eating.

If you consciously check in throughout a meal, there will come a juncture when you're aware that you've had about enough to eat. You could stop, or you could take another few bites. As an experiment, go ahead and try one more bite. Now assess how you feel—was it one bite too many, or was it just right? If you stay conscious in this way, you become aware of a most curious thing. When you eat more than you need, the food doesn't taste as good as it did when you were hungry. When you notice the flavor of the food diminishing, that's a clue that you've had enough to satisfy yourself.

With repeated practice and consciousness, you'll become sensitive to your point of satisfaction. If you're consciously tuning into your feedback, it simply won't feel good to overeat. It's important to remember that the goal isn't to try to eat until you're full— you're trying to eat until you're satisfied.

There's an important difference between satisfaction and fullness. Being satisfied is when your hunger has been appeased. Being full means that you've eaten more than you need. Even when you're full, it's possible to keep eating and get even more full. At Thanksgiving, when you've had all you need to eat before you've even started the main course, you just unzip the pants and keep on going. Satisfied hunger happens right before you're full—it's a feeling of completeness without excess.

strategy 5: learn how to admit that too little is too little: At the other end of the spectrum, you may have fallen into a pattern of eating less and less, to the point of severe undernourishment. What started out as an effort to lose weight has eroded into a dangerous habit of denying your hunger altogether. In that case, you must admit to yourself that undereating has gone too far. You need to refamiliarize yourself with your body's signs of genuine hunger.

If you're in the habit of starving yourself, eating anything at all may seem like a huge threat. You may eat only if you're in a social situation that forces you to, or because you'll pass out if you don't. This method of ignoring hunger may have proven initially "successful" for you—you lost weight, perhaps lots of weight. But undereating won't bring you closer to true happiness. In fact, it will keep you trapped in a convoluted and painful relationship with your body.

Undereating can be a complicated pattern to break. You may feel that you can't give it up because it keeps you thin, and you fear the inevitable weight gain that will come with a return to eating. Lack of food also impairs your judgment. You may feel you're in control of the situation, but when you're light-headed, even high, from too few calories, you can't think straight.

When undereating has gone this far, it's no longer an issue of weight control. Starvation is dangerous because of the potential for

long-lasting physical and psychological damage. If you find it hard
to resolve your undereating issues, the best thing you can do is to
find someone to help you, preferably a reputable therapist who
specializes in eating disorders.

You must also do some work on your own. You can start to
make immediate changes by tuning into your feedback. Begin by
paying attention to your hunger. It may initially feel overwhelming, but if you can hang in there and remain conscious, you will
learn how to respond appropriately to your hunger.

When you've fallen out of the whole realm of eating, there's
also a physical component that keeps you stuck. You may no
longer even salivate at the thought of delicious food. When you're
out of practice, that first bite of food doesn't carry any aesthetic
appeal. In fact, it can be deeply terrifying because you know that if
you start eating again, your game of "effortless" thinness is over.

But if you can bring yourself to eat anything at all, you can start
to get your physical system up and running. At first you may experience extreme hunger. Once those floodgates are open, it may feel
as though you'll be swept away by your desire to eat. Here's where
paying attention to your feedback and your hunger level will save
you. By remaining mindful and conscious, watching your swings
between hunger and denial of hunger, you'll eventually find your
way to balance.

At this stage, the preceding conscious strategies will help you understand your true hunger. Pay close attention to what foods you like to eat. Eat consciously, and savor your food. Carefully assess when you're full, and stop eating when you've had enough. Take it slowly, moment by moment—you will learn how to trust yourself again.

strategy 6: the choice is yours: When you're in a pattern of eating without mindfulness, your unconscious state doesn't allow for many choices. You eat according to habits and patterns, rather than actively responding to your hunger.

But when you respond to your hunger and eat consciously, you have choices to make. Because you're familiar with your own internal gauge for hunger, you'll know when it's time to stop eating. But that doesn't mean you'll necessarily *choose* to stop eating. Sometimes you may still choose to overeat; if you do, so be it. But now, with your conscious eating practice, you'll be watching yourself every step along the way. You'll consciously observe the whole cycle: the excitement that builds before you eat, the pleasure as you eat, and the eventual discomfort and disappointment that follows overeating.

After this kind of eating episode, you may experience self-recrimination, beating yourself up for having pigged out. But with consciousness, you'll be able to bring compassion to your situation. Your behavior may still feel painful and abusive. But in the light of consciousness, which keeps your personal purpose before you, you'll be able to forgive yourself—and move on.

Making choices that feel supportive of your sense of purpose isn't a matter of forcing yourself to do the "right thing"—to never pig out again, never touch a granule of sugar, and generally lead a chaste and pious life. When faced with the prospect of doing that kind of right thing, we picture a horribly boring, self-denying, drab, colorless existence. But the choices that bring you lasting happiness aren't drab and colorless, even though they might seem in total contrast to your former sense of a good time. The difference is that you're no longer looking outside of yourself for that elusive source of happiness. Eventually you'll want to make choices that feel good to you. It's a matter of learning what you want deep down.

unconscious habits and nagging urges

Some days your sense of hunger can become easily confused by the murky lines separating true hunger, habitual patterns, and urges. Hunger, habits, and urges are so deeply intertwined that separating them is challenging.

We define *habits* as ingrained, unconscious behaviors. The unconsciousness of an act is precisely what makes it a habit. As you've discovered, unconsciousness is the root cause of habitual eating, and consciousness is the antidote.

Chewing your food on the left side of your mouth, strapping on your seat belt, or having tea every afternoon are all examples of habits. Not all habits are bad. In fact, many are beneficial and can make your life easier. But all food habits, whether or not you consider them to be beneficial, need to be brought to consciousness.

Unlike habits, an urge is something you're overtly aware of. Urges burst on the scene, grabbing your attention with an *urgent* call to action. They can, of course, be intertwined with habits—it's the time of day when you always have your diet cola, and an alarm blasts inside informing you to go and get it *now*. Urges can also be driven by hunger, often when you haven't acknowledged it. For example, you've been slaving away at the computer for hours, skipping lunch, when suddenly you sit upright drooling for a candy bar.

When we get an urge, our more "responsible" self can chime in and say, "Not now, it's not good to eat that food at this time of day." Any respectable urge, hearing that sort of discouragement, does what urges do best—it pushes harder and louder until it eventually wins, or a frustrating tug-of-war ensues between the conflicting internal forces.

What can be difficult about working with urges is their strong connection to our emotions. The nature of an urge is to be satisfied immediately. Like children, when we get an urge for something, we *really want it no matter what.* Not getting it hurts. On the flip side, getting it brings us a measure of happiness, no matter how fleeting. When we have an urge, we're not thinking about the fact that our pleasure may quickly turn into dismay.

being whole

For many women, food habits and urges can seem frightening or even demonic. We just can't seem to keep them under control, like some sort of twisted jack-in-the-box that bursts the lid and frightens us. We shun these habits and urges, abhor them, or run away from them. Try as we may, it always seems that our bad habits and undignified urges sabotage all our sincere efforts to make changes.

Whether we like to admit it or not, everything we do, think, and feel—habits and urges included—is part of the fabric that makes up who we are. We fear or loathe some parts of ourselves and prefer the "nicer" parts. This keeps us willfully ignorant of who we are as a whole person.

By purposely remaining blind to these shameful, darker parts of ourselves, we become enslaved by the very parts we won't acknowledge. Those ugly blemishes you'd rather not have to see are just as much a part of you as the "good girl." That's not to say that the dark part of ourselves is in any way a permanent, indelible part of our makeup. Everything is subject to change. By acknowledging and owning our whole selves, we can be the ones to direct change toward our sense of purpose.

PRACTICE: CONSCIOUS STRATEGIES—
HABITS AND URGES

strategy 1: ask yourself if you're hungry: When you notice a food urge or habit, you might actually be hungry. Stop momentarily and check for your personal signs of hunger, which you previously identified. Don't forget to look for signs of thirst as well. If you are in fact hungry, go back to the strategies for discovering how to satisfy your true hunger.

strategy 2: delay gratification: Sometimes, when you feel hungry, you find yourself enmeshed in a conflict between your true hunger and an urge. When you check in with your body, you may hear two different messages: one saying that a nectarine would taste great, and the other urging you to wolf down a cheese Danish as fast as you can—before you change your mind.

If you feel conflicted about what to eat, put some time between you and your urge. Avoid taking immediate action on it. Can you stand to delay your gratification by a minute, thirty minutes, or indefinitely?

A good framework for delaying gratification is to set a time limit (the actual time is up to you, just make it reasonable): "I'll give myself thirty minutes, and if I still want to eat the food at the end of that time, I may." If you're still not sure whether to eat the food when the time arrives, set a new time limit. Continue with this strategy until you decide to eat the food, or until the urge goes away.

When you delay gratification, it's important to also acknowledge that you *can* eat the food right now if you want to. If you instead tell yourself "no," a battle ensues within. By giving yourself permission, as well as some time, you can sidestep your internal battle.

If you decide to give in to the urge and eat the food, do so with one qualifier: that you'll eat it consciously. Sometimes the only thing that will satisfy an urge is to eat at least a bite of whatever food is calling you. At those times, if you don't take at least one bite, you'll eat every healthy and not so healthy crumb in the house because you haven't had what you really desire. If you decide to go ahead and eat the food, take it bite by bite, checking with each mouthful to see if your urge is now satisfied. Conscious observation will give you valuable insight into how this urge may be part of your habitual food patterns.

The goal of this strategy certainly isn't to eat whatever you want whenever you want. Rather, it's to find a balanced way to work with the complexity of your urges. When you work with urges, you can't stifle them, but you can't run whole hog with them, either. The middle path to working with urges is consciousness. Consciousness allows you to pay sincere attention to an urge and gives you the perspective you need to make an informed and considered choice.

strategy 3: what's the worst and best that could happen?: If you're having trouble deciding whether to give in to an urge, another good strategy is to ask yourself two simple questions: "What's the worst that can happen if I follow my desire?" and "What's the best that can happen?"

Contemplating these opposing questions can be very powerful. For example, perhaps you're thinking about eating your favorite candy. The worst that could happen might be that you eat all of the candy in the house, rush out and get more, and eat so much that you wind up in the emergency room. That's bad, but highly unlikely. The best that could happen might be that you eat some of the candy and realize partway through your first bag that you've had enough, and stop eating.

By envisioning the extremes of what might happen, you create perspective for yourself and disengage from fear. Often we're so blocked by fear that we're incapable of checking in with our feedback. By giving yourself permission to contemplate the best and the worst results, you can free yourself to make a more rational decision.

strategy 4: everything's up for grabs: It's difficult to see hidden habits, such as eating quickly, eating while doing something else, or eating the same foods repeatedly. For women, the dieting mentality has created many of our hidden habits. We weigh and measure our foods, thinking in terms of fat content, protein, or carbohydrates. We relegate some foods to the off-limits category while labeling others as safe. These "healthy" habits that we develop in an attempt to lose weight may in fact be doing us the most harm.

All habits are unconscious, patterned behaviors. If you're to know what you personally need to eat, *all* of your habits are up for grabs. You must bring conscious consideration to even your most cherished habits, your personal sacred cows.

For instance, you never, ever eat potato chips because they're high in fat and you believe they put weight on you instantly. Or you're very hungry after an especially active day, and you stop at the four ounces of chicken you always allot yourself, even though you feel as if you could eat twice that amount to feel satisfied.

These habits may have been formed with the best of intentions. But because they've become unconscious behaviors themselves, they could be the very habits keeping you stuck. Therefore, you need to examine all of your food behaviors and thoughts. Your most cherished healthy habits may be blocking your feedback, preventing you from trusting yourself to know how much and what to eat.

Rather than weighing and measuring your dinner portion, try visually filling your own plate with the amount of food that feels appropriate. Then eat slowly and with consciousness until satisfied but not full (see "Conscious Strategies—Hunger," numbers 3 and 4, pages 181 and 184). If you can learn to trust your feedback, you'll find that you can let go of the false security that these kinds of healthy habits provide.

You may also find that some habits are beneficial behaviors. But instead of continuing on with them unconsciously, you'll employ them consciously. For instance, you may automatically avoid all foods with high fat content. But with conscious eating, you might decide to limit foods with a high fat content because you've noticed that you consistently feel sluggish after eating them. Outwardly it may seem like the same behavior: avoiding fat. But the difference is that now you'll make an active, conscious choice to avoid fat based on your feedback.

strategy 5: take responsibility: The one great thing about food habits is that they free us of the onerous responsibility of thinking for ourselves about what we should eat. So when we consider giving up habits, we're faced with the prospect of doing the hard work of making our own decisions.

When we no longer mindlessly employ habitual guidelines to tell us what to eat, we're saddled with our own decisions and behavior. With our newfound freedom comes newfound responsibility.

A good example of needing to balance freedom with personal responsibility was the "diets don't work" counterrevolution that emerged several years ago. The basic idea, with all good intention, was to shift away from programmed, habitual dieting behaviors.

Many pent-up dieters heard the message that diets don't work and knew it to be true. Finally freed from the repression of rules they'd followed for years, they tossed away their diets and went on an all-out binge. When the pounds piled on, many of these same people returned grudgingly—and perhaps disillusioned—to follow the safe boundaries set by diets.

Diets *don't* work, but neither does mindlessly throwing all rules out the window. There's a middle path between these two extremes called consciousness. Without rules, you must follow the messages of your own feedback. You can give up the diet and the unconscious behaviors associated with it. But in return you must take up the responsibility of consciousness.

We must decide, like the adults we are, what foods are right for us and how much of those foods we should eat. And if our choices turn out to be wrong, if the foods we choose make us feel ill or we eat more than we need, then that's a learning experience. Balancing freedom with responsibility gives us an increased understanding of our bodies and our nutritional needs.

Responsibility does require effort and commitment. But when you've seen the other side—replacing your responsibility with a diet that never works—reclaiming your life becomes a joy.

strategy 6: don't try to exterminate the habit—just try to know it: Often we rush headlong into kicking the habit before we even know what the habit is. For instance, we know we eat too much chocolate, so we decide to stop that habit altogether. But our habits can provide extremely useful information about what's going on beneath the surface. Why do we eat chocolate? What times of day do we eat it? What else is going on in our lives when it's chocolate time? What does our feedback tell us before we eat chocolate, as we eat it, a few hours later, the next day? As we observe ourselves with mindfulness while we eat the chocolate, what can we learn?

Rushing to kick the habit can actually evolve into just another unconscious habit. We swing from extreme to extreme: binge on chocolate; eat no chocolate! The point is not to give up all habits immediately. Instead, we want to observe our habits and come to understand their roots.

Your intention should be to simply observe your own behaviors in their natural habitat. Not so you can stomp them out—just so you can watch them with compassion. By getting to know your own habits, you'll have a much better understanding of where you are right now—start where you are. That way you can rationally and consciously decide how to respond to future urges.

strategy 7: avoid the obvious traps: Working skillfully with habits and urges can be a lot like working with a child. An artful tactic for redirecting unruly behavior in children is to try to make sure that the opportunity for misbehavior doesn't arise. Similarly, a good way to undo habits is to avoid setting up opportunities for them to arise.

If, for example, you consistently lose control over a certain food, you might consider not stocking it in your pantry. Or if you know you always eat and drink too much when you go out with certain friends, you might decline their next invitation.

This type of solution can be helpful because it removes the temptation and gives you some space until you feel more resolved in your food practices. But ultimately, it's only a temporary solution, because it doesn't require you to work with your consciousness and sense of purpose.

As you start out with your food practices, avoid situations that make you feel out of control. This can help to provide the safe environment you need for making changes. Use the space to strengthen your ability to remain conscious and in touch with your feedback.

strategy 8: unmask the demon: We often have one food habit or urge that seems so intense, shameful, or debilitating that we think it's unresolvable. We fear that it will always haunt us, destroying our best efforts to eat sanely. We try everything possible to put a stop to this food behavior. But like a demon lurking within us, it just waits for an opportunity to pull us wildly out of control.

This kind of a food urge is distinguished by always seeming to escalate into behavior that feels out of control. Perhaps it's an urge that results in a mindless state of nonstop eating until we're so full we feel ill. Or it may be an urge that launches us on a cycle of overeating followed by repentant fasting for days on end. Whatever form it takes, it's *the* habitual behavior that we know in our heart is our most shameful dark secret about food and body.

First of all, you need to acknowledge this part of yourself. By doing so, you can put it into the proper perspective. This food behavior is just one part of all the many elements that go into making up your whole—it's by no means all of you. But when you fear it and keep it a secret, the power it accrues while hiding in the dark greatly increases its seeming magnitude.

Your demonic pattern comes and goes, just like any other part of you. And just like any habit, it's not necessarily one you're destined to carry for the rest of your life. But right now it's there, and it's real.

Once you've identified the demonic urge and ensuing pattern, the next step is to watch it. Don't try to change it; simply observe it. At first this might just mean that when the urge arises, you think, "Oh no! That horrible feeling." Sometime after you've repeated the unspeakable pattern of behavior, you might think, "I had the urge, and here I am, disgusted with myself on the other side of it. Yuck!"

But if you maintain your commitment to bringing awareness to the habit, you'll reach a point where you can observe the entire pattern from beginning to end. Eventually, if you really don't like the pattern—if it makes you feel imbalanced or unhealthy, if it's destructive to your peace of mind, if it draws you way from your ability to experience your sense of purpose—then you simply won't want to do it anymore. Your commitment to consciousness will resolve this problem.

jumping off the treadmill

As you continue with the food practices and apply strategies to staying conscious, your eating will change over time. You won't exert your willpower, you won't starve, you won't choose one food group over another as your new weight-loss magic bullet. Instead, you'll learn to eat what you're hungry for. By exercising your aesthetic sense and judging foods using your sensitive inner meter, you'll find that you don't eat based on any external standards for health. Rather, you'll eat the foods that you prefer, and that feel healthy to you. In this way, consciousness becomes its own reward. Although being conscious requires us to be aware of unpleasant or painful things, the reward is that it allows you to be authentic. You can finally be exactly who you are.

There's an old saying: "You can run but you can't hide." We may spend an entire lifetime running from the truth of who we are. But it's so much more deeply and ultimately rewarding to stop running, to just stop all of the games, and simply see ourselves as we are right now.

TEN

you are a work in progress

What are these Four Noble Truths? They are the noble truth of suffering; the noble truth of the origin of suffering; the noble truth of the end of suffering; and the noble truth of the way to the end of suffering.

—THE BUDDHA

When we go to sleep at night, we become unconscious. We're unaware of our surroundings as we dissolve into another realm and dream away. But when we wake up in the morning and find ourselves returned to our familiar place in the world, does that mean we're fully conscious?

Most of us wake up into another kind of dream—the dream of

our lives. Sleepwalking through life is the natural state of affairs. So much of life escapes our notice. We go from moment to moment lost in an oblivion of habits, musings, and daydreams, taking actions and making choices that we're only half aware of, if at all.

There's a deeper level of waking up that can be achieved. It's the type of waking up we've been exploring throughout this book, which comes from honing our consciousness. By waking up through greater conscious awareness, we can end our food and body madness once and for all. We can hop off the not-so-merry-go-round of dieting, self-criticism, and deprivation.

The great accomplishment of the Buddha that separates him from other human beings is that he woke up—became conscious—within his life. The term "Buddha" literally means "one who is awake," from the root "budh," which means "to wake up."

The Jataka tales, which tell the stories of the Buddha's many lifetimes, demonstrate how the Buddha fought heroically to awaken ever more fully. His ultimate battle to become fully awake was against the Great Tempter, Mara. Mara sent everything he had to prevent the Buddha from fully awakening—desires to seduce him and terrors to frighten him. But the Buddha held steadfast.

As he became more fully awake, he could see that because all things pass and change with time, everything Mara could use against him was purely illusory—it had no permanent substance. He saw that all things are subject to change: the things we love and the things we hate. Being awake to these noble truths, he could see that the pleasures that Mara offered him, as well as the pain, were only ephemeral moments. These, too, would soon pass and transform, just like everything else. He knew he had nothing to fear or gain from these ever changing illusions. This realization was the ultimate insight, and he became fully awakened.

the changing nature of obstacles

It's the nature of life that all things change. A child matures, a wound heals, and spring transforms into summer. Yet it's human nature to want things to remain organized, fixed, and unchanging. We want to make things look like the picture of what we desire them to be, rather than appreciating the essence of what they are right now.

As longtime dieters, we both long for and flee from change. We want to change the crazy way we eat, change our bodies, change which clothes fit, and change all of the mirrors so they're much more complimentary. But when we've managed to make positive changes, such as losing weight, we want to put a grinding halt to change and keep things the way they are forever.

Wanting things to stay the same when they can't will present an obstacle to your happiness. If you're following a diet and it no longer works, you become unhappy. Similarly, if you're trusting your feedback and sense of purpose to guide you and they no longer seem to work, you may rush off in search of a new formula. But the difference between your past diets and what you've learned in this book is that Western diets are external, mechanistic solutions that can't allow for the tide of change.

From an Eastern point of view, the fact that all things change is one of the most fundamental reasons to renew and reinvigorate your efforts to wake up. If you're prepared for the types of obstacles you may run into, and if you can face them with conscious awareness, you'll discover that they present an opportunity to guide your own course of change.

PRACTICE: COMMON OBSTACLES—AND WHAT TO DO ABOUT THEM

obstacle 1: conscious—who, me?: The first obstacle you'll encounter is forgetting to be conscious. You set out with all good intention to eat a meal or do your sitting meditation practice with awareness. And the next thing you know, the food on your plate is all gone, or forty-five minutes has flown by on the clock, and where were you?

Loss of consciousness is going to happen. Not once or twice, but actually more often than not. It's very difficult to remain conscious—even for twenty seconds. The force of a lifetime of habitual unconsciousness can't be instantly replaced with pure, focused consciousness. But when you wake up at any given moment and realize you've been unconscious, you can instantly become conscious. That you are conscious for even a moment is infinitely better than never being conscious.

Like anything else you do in life, staying conscious for longer periods of time becomes easier the more you practice it. So to face this first obstacle, you can practice staying conscious. Do the meditation and yoga practices outlined in Chapter Seven, and allow yourself to consciously observe the resulting feelings, sensations, and thoughts. Since all of the practices work on progressively deepening your conscious awareness, repeat these as well. The more time you spend in that place of consciousness, the easier you'll find it to stay there for longer intervals. It will also get easier to tune back into your consciousness when you inevitably lose it again.

obstacle 2: I got it—I don't got it: Another obstacle you'll meet is your ego, and its strong desire to be finished with all of this learning and evolution. When the techniques in this book start to work, and you experience some relief, you may really start to think, "I've got it. It all makes sense, I know what it's all about, and—problem solved."

It's very helpful to appreciate the progress you've made. But as soon as you think you finally have it figured out, that thought alone should set off a big red light warning you of impending unconsciousness. There's a well-known passage in Indian philosophy that can serve as your guiding insight: "They who think they know it know it not" (Kena Upanishad I. 1–3).

So when the triumphant thought arises that you've got this thing figured out, whether during your yoga practice or as you sit down to eat a meal, simply be aware that you may be slipping out of mindful awareness of the present moment. This obstacle is easy to recognize if you're willing to suspend your ego long enough to recall, "Oh yeah, when I think that I've got it, doesn't that mean just the opposite?"

The good news and the bad news is we need to keep going deeper all the time, because change and time won't let us stand still. What we "get" today doesn't quite encompass what we meet tomorrow. The point isn't to finally arrive and get it once and for all—it's to keep on learning as we travel the path of change.

obstacle 3: just add water: It can be frightening when your old patterns and habits suddenly reappear as if they were freeze-dried and lying in wait just below the surface. You thought (or maybe prayed) that they were gone forever, but now they're back, and they're threatening to take over. A seemingly insignificant incident or state of mind sets them off. Just add water and they come back to life, as unhealthy and troubling as ever.

For example, you may have had insight into the concept that your looks aren't the center of meaning for you. Then you happen to pass by a shop window and catch a glimpse of yourself. Without warning, you plummet back into a state of self-criticism that you thought you'd left behind long ago in the bad old days. This sort of rebounding into an old pattern can happen at any time and can be triggered by anything.

Just knowing that your "worst" habits are likely to resurface is the first step in working through this obstacle. Remember that it probably took years for the patterns to develop in the first place. Your old food and body habits are just as much a part of you as anything else; it takes time to work through their depths.

Instead of despairing at your inability to make changes, just hang in there and remain conscious as you watch your old nemeses reappear. If you don't actively allow yourself to go off into a torrent of self-judgment and criticism, the habit will lose its former power to overwhelm you. You'll be able to see that it's just a pattern that will pass, and can hook you in only if you buy into it.

You can also get proactive when meeting this obstacle by returning to the "Conscious Strategies" section of Chapter Nine (page 178). These strategies will help you to recognize the structure and difficulties of food and body habits. When you consciously forge new patterns that you feel attracted to, your old patterns will eventually just become old memories. When they resurface, you'll shake your head and wonder why they were ever so beguiling.

obstacle 4: the swing of the pendulum: As you continue with the practices in this book, you may find that you lose weight, feel increased energy, and enjoy an overall greatly improved sense of fitness. How can you help but enjoy this improved set of circumstances? You may well feel a sense of pride that you've made such positive changes in your life without resorting to the old, painful tricks of dieting and deprivation.

But as you go on, and your body adjusts to these initial positive changes, you may find that there comes a day when you reach a plateau. What's the matter? Haven't you been following the practices? Aren't you in touch with your personal purpose anymore? Aren't you being conscious when you eat? With no seeming reason, you're no longer enjoying the same results. What went wrong?

Because our bodies and our life circumstances change over time, what worked yesterday may not work today. We refer to this as the swing of the pendulum. For example, you follow the all-carb diet because you hear it's low-calorie and provides great energy. At first it works great. Eventually, however, you no longer feel good, and you start gaining weight. Then you hear about the new high-protein diet. You toss away your carbs, eat the bacon and the burger without the bun, and it works—for a while. But you can bet good money that sooner or later, the pendulum will swing again, and your new approach will stop working. It's inevitable that, given enough time, your body will shift, and you'll have to accommodate these changes if you're to remain healthy and balanced. If you're plateauing, try asking yourself the following questions: "Has consciousness become a new kind of habit?" "Have these practices become just another routine?"

You may think that you're being conscious as you do a practice. You sit down to your meal, quickly set your intention, and check in several times with your feedback as you eat. You think, "Hearing feedback, being conscious." But you've turned the process into a kind of a mental shorthand, reciting those words without really being present. This is similar to the obstacle of thinking we've got it. Because we know *how* to be conscious and full of purpose when we eat, we assume we don't have to work at it anymore.

But consciousness requires constant work. When your body is giving you the clear signal that it needs something new, or you need to tune in more deeply, consciousness is the only tool that will help you know what you need. It can be discouraging if you start gaining weight or feel unhealthy after starting to feel good again. You may feel like all of your hard work and success have gone down the drain. But there are many levels of success, and many levels of satisfaction.

If your energy or health doesn't feel balanced, or you're gaining unwanted weight, then it's time to approach the practices anew. Try to do the practices as if you've never done them before. Most important, reexamine your intention for wanting to make changes. With a fresh, newly inspired intention, the practices and their benefits will be renewed.

Finding your way through this common obstacle won't always be easy. But you know diets and deprivation don't work, so you have no choice but to continue to find another way. The honest search for meaning and purpose, through the vehicle of consciousness, is the only way to really know yourself.

obstacle 5: the truth or not the truth?: Doubt can be a huge obstacle in and of itself. You may question your ability to know what's right or wrong, especially when you're learning to trust your instincts.

Your self-doubt may be augmented by mistakes you've made in the past: thinking you were marrying the right person, leaping at a job that turned out to be dreadful, or getting into debt over your head. At the time, you may have thought you were considering all the right angles before going forward. When it all turned out wrong a few years later, you may have wondered how your instincts could have been so bad.

Doubts about what you should eat and how you should exercise may also arise. For example, if you lose weight, and then your weight plateaus, you may think you *can't* trust yourself to intuitively know what feels balanced and healthy. Or someone might tell you that intuitive eating sounds stupid and they have a much better diet for you. Again you may doubt your instincts. You wonder—is it enough that what you're doing feels right on an instinctual level, and you feel happier?

Keep in mind that it takes practice to really trust yourself. Most women with a food and body conflict are by definition out of practice. Most are also extremely self-critical. We blame ourselves for the mess we're in, for every bite we take, for every diet that's failed. We're at fault, and we're always apprehensive of the next horrible thing we'll do to ourselves.

When you're self-critical, doubting yourself is an entrenched habit. But in fact, only *you* can know what's best for you. How you know what's best for you is a matter of evaluating each situation individually. You consider your own feedback (primarily your gut instinct), the facts of the situation, and input from others. Weighing all of these factors, you'll be able to decide what's right for you.

Trusting yourself isn't a matter of tossing away the reins of your responsibility. Trust requires that you judge your actions from many different viewpoints, not only your gut instinct. As with any decision in your life, your powers of reason and your sense of ethical responsibility are still equally important.

It's inevitable that you'll make mistakes; that's one of the risks of trusting yourself. But if you make a mistake, or if things don't turn out exactly as planned, it's an opportunity to learn. Rather than leaping to the conclusion that you can't trust yourself at all, you'll learn that you *can* trust yourself to make midcourse corrections.

obstacle 6: what's this spirituality stuff?: As we make changes, our relationships with others are also bound to change. In the past, you may have found your friends and family to be unsupportive of your dieting efforts. That may pale in comparison to the difficulties you could experience when you decide that you want to live a more meaningful and spiritual life.

In many Eastern cultures, spirituality is an integral part of everyday life. But here in the West, we pride ourselves on separation of church and state. Our everyday lives show this separation between spirituality—and everything else. Not everyone you encounter will believe that spirituality is of any importance at all. Some people may not believe in such a concept as spirituality, whereas others may actually find it threatening. They may deride you for caring about something so nontangible, criticize you for abandoning your more sensible self, or worry that you've joined a cult. Dealing with their disapproval can be especially difficult when they're your friends and family.

But the flip side is, *you* may be the one who's judging others on how they choose to live. You may disapprove if they live a life that you consider to be generally lacking in meaning. You may want to show them the error of their ways and help them to make the same kinds of changes that have made you so much happier.

But just as you'd like your loved ones to be tolerant, it's equally important to be genuinely respectful of others. You probably don't like to be told how to live your life, and neither does anyone else. Even when we really, *really* think we know better about how someone ought to live his or her life, our intended audience probably won't welcome our "sharing" that information.

When your relationships are based on mutual respect—even though you may not pursue the same path of spirituality or meaning—you'll be able to reach an understanding. You'll eventually come to see that you're different people with different approaches to life. And if some fundamental differences remain, you can agree to disagree.

But if your friends or loved ones can't respect or tolerate your personal choices, then you need to consider these relationships closely. What do you enjoy about the relationship, and what isn't working for you? If you come to the conclusion that your relationship isn't supportive, you may reach the painful juncture of deciding whether or not to continue with it.

If a relationship is harmful and hinders your ability to pursue meaning and evolve, then it may be time to end it. When you're contemplating these kinds of issues, the assistance of a good thera- pist can be essential.

obstacle 7: where did my purpose go?: There may come a time when you find yourself questioning what holds meaning for you. You may specifically ponder your personal purpose and wonder if it's still relevant to your life. This obstacle can go something like this: as you do the practices, you're able to get in touch with your sense of personal purpose, and you find it incredibly inspiring. When difficulties arise, you're able to stay connected to your pur- pose, and it carries you sailing through the hard times. You feel in- credibly "high" as your life starts to change for the better.

Then one day you try to tap into your personal purpose but find that you don't feel so inspired. You try again, in an effort to squeeze the old juice out of it, hoping to find the comfort and peace that it once brought you. But nothing happens. You try repeatedly, but the well seems to have run dry. What happened?

Because everything is subject to change, even our sense of pur- pose or spirituality may change, too. The purpose that once filled us with inspiration may now seem empty and meaningless. When you meet this obstacle, you may be tempted to junk the whole process and go back to your old unconscious ways.

First of all, don't panic! You haven't lost your way, it's just time to take your sense of purpose to the next level. Revisit Chapter Three and the practices for "Finding Your Personal Purpose" (see page 42). As you do them again, drop all preconceptions about what your purpose *should* be or was the last time you did the practice. Explore openly and honestly what holds meaning for you right now. You'll no doubt find that your original sense of purpose was just the initial layer that was accessible to you at the time.

Don't be afraid to go continually deeper, letting go of your old ideals and allowing new ones to arise. This process of change is how we continue to mature and evolve. Having a crisis of purpose doesn't mean that we don't know what we want in life—it means that we've got enough faith to honestly explore what we *do* want in life.

healing moment by moment

The path we've taken you on throughout this book has been one of healing. We haven't given you a magic formula that will solve your food and body conflict—we wish we could. Instead, we've shown you the door that can take you within, the door into conscious-ness. Behind this door awaits a journey of self-discovery and healing where you'll find peace of mind, and an existence inspired by your personal sense of purpose.

It's here—awake in each moment—that you can start to heal your food and body conflict. When you've been stuck for so long, it seems that food and body will always be your focus. But the practices can release you from your place of conflict and bring you instead to a place of balance and healing.

An essential part of this healing is the practice of self-inquiry. Self-inquiry is the act of looking inside of ourselves and questioning all that we see. This questioning is a method of examining the present moment. You ask yourself, "How am I today?" and you get back an answer: "Not so good," "Great," "Kind of sleepy." This brief process has just given you vital information about yourself.

To deepen your inquiry, you continue with the self-questioning: "Why aren't I so good today?" You might hear a surprising answer: "Because I'm depressed that I have so much work to do." By questioning all of your answers, you can go on and on until you feel that you've drilled down to the actual root of your experience. As you continue to question yourself in this way, you go ever deeper on your journey through the doors of consciousness. You get a glimpse into the deep roots of your being. When you question yourself openly, honestly, and lovingly—not looking for answers, simply looking for more questions—you begin to heal.

Self-inquiry is a call to question everything. It is not self-criticism or rejecting your beliefs. Instead, it is the art of honestly observing even the subtlest aspects of your existence: your inner life as well as your personal actions in the world. It is a methodology that allows you to be starkly honest with yourself. By doing so, you can finally start getting to the root of the genuine issues that keep you stuck. The more you continue with the process, the more you'll learn what's really going on inside of you. Self-inquiry questions even the very questions that you're asking—nothing is left out of the inquiry.

the wake-up call

When you've been sleepwalking through life for a long time, you may suddenly receive a wake-up call. In a flash, you realize that somewhere along the line, you got lost in your life. You headed down the wrong path, going against your gut sense of right and wrong. When you get the wake-up call, you know that you've got a choice: make some changes or continue on your destructive path. It's a call to see the truth, and act on it, before it's too late.

The food and body conflict that caused you to pick up this book can serve as your wake-up call. It's trying desperately to get your attention. It's your call to reawaken to your own inner truth. As you follow that call and continue to heal, you'll awaken to deeper and deeper truths. The real reward is not only finding balance in food and body but discovering your own passion for pursuing meaning. The unexpected gift of your food and body conflict is that it can bring you back home.

When we arrive at home, we realize there is no place truly like it. Home is where we belong, it's who we are, it's our truth. As the poet John Keats said, "'Beauty is truth, truth is beauty,'— that is all/Ye know on earth, and all ye need to know." When we accept our whole selves, we awaken to *our* truth, and to our own beauty.

All of the practices contained in this book are methods for discovering your own truth and your own beauty. These practices each hold a part of the solution to your food and body conflict; they each help you to spend more of your time in a state of consciousness. The more time you spend conscious and connected to your personal sense of spirituality, the more opportunity you'll have for change. By keeping what's most meaningful to you in the forefront of your mind, and by learning to recognize your body's signs of balance, you'll make the right choices for you in any given moment. When you're in the trenches of your day-to-day struggle with food and your body, you'll have the polestar of your own sense of meaning and conscious awareness to help you find your way.

From the wake-up call of your food and body conflict to finding your way back home, you're on a journey of discovery. The point is not to arrive anywhere. It's to continue on your path as you seek the greatest reward—to uncover the meaning that lies hidden within each and every moment. You are a work in progress.

suggested resources

YOGA BOOKS

Desikachar, T. K. V. *The Heart of Yoga: Developing a Personal Practice.*
Rochester, Vt.: Inner Traditions, 1999.

Farhi, Donna. *Yoga Mind, Body and Spirit: A Return to Wholeness.* New
York: Henry Holt, 2000.

Iyengar, B. K. S. *Light on Yoga,* rev. ed. New York: Schocken Books,
1995.

———. *The Tree of Yoga.* Boston: Shambhala, 1989.

Schiffmann, Erich. *Yoga: The Spirit and Practice of Moving into Stillness.*
New York: Pocket Books, 1996.

Swenson, David. *Ashtanga Yoga "The Practice Manual."* Sugar Land, Tex.: Ashtanga Yoga Productions, 1999.

Yee, Rodney, with Nina Zolotow. *Yoga: The Poetry of the Body.* New York: St. Martin's Press, 2002.

EASTERN PHILOSOPHY

Doniger, Wendy. *Splitting the Difference: Gender and Myth in Ancient Greece and India.* Chicago: University of Chicago Press, 1999.

Hahn, Thich Nhat. *The Heart of the Buddha's Teaching: Transforming Suffering into Peace, Joy and Liberation.* New York: Broadway Books, 1999.

Olivelle, Patrick, trans. *Upanishads (Oxford World Classics).* New York: Oxford University Press, 1998.

Radhakrishnan, Sarvepalli, and Charles A. Moore, ed. *A Source Book in Indian Philosophy.* Princeton, N.J.: Princeton University Press, 1967.

MEDITATION BOOKS

Goldstein, Joseph, and Jack Kornfield. *Seeking the Heart of Wisdom: The Path of Insight Meditation.* Boston: Shambhala, 2001.

Hahn, Thich Nhat. *The Miracle of Mindfulness: A Manual on Meditation.* Boston: Beacon Press, 1996.

Suzuki, Shunryu. *Zen Mind, Beginner's Mind.* Trumbull, Conn.: Weatherhill, 1988.

NUTRITION/COOKING

Colbin, Annemarie. *Food and Healing.* New York: Ballantine Books, 1996.

Robbins, John. *The Food Revolution: How Your Diet Can Change Your Life and Our World.* Berkeley: Conari Press, 2001.

Taylor, Mary F. *Lunch Crunch: Beating the Lunch Box Blues.* Boulder, Colo.: Yoga Workshop Press, 1997.

————. *New Vegetarian Classics: Entrees.* Santa Cruz, Calif.: Crossing Press, 1994.

————. *New Vegetarian Classics: Soups.* Santa Cruz, Calif.: Crossing Press, 1996.

Tiwari, Maya. *Ayurveda—A Life of Balance.* Rochester, Vt.: Inner Traditions, 1995.

Willett, Walter C. *Eat, Drink, and Be Healthy: The Harvard Medical School Guide to Healthy Eating.* New York: Simon & Schuster, 2001.

VIDEO

Freeman, Richard. *Yoga Breathing and Relaxation with Richard Freeman.* Boulder, Colo.: Delphi Productions.

————. *Yoga with Richard Freeman: Ashtanga Yoga: The Primary Series.* Boulder, Colo.: Delphi Productions.

suggested reading

Kornfield, Jack. *Meditation for Beginners.* Louisville, Colo.: Sounds True.

Macgraw, Ali. *Ali Macgraw—Yoga Mind and Body.* Warner Studios.

Yee, Rodney, and Patricia Walden. *Living Yoga—A.M./P.M. Yoga for Beginners Set.* Broomfield, Colo.: Living Arts.

AUDIOTAPES

Freeman, Richard. *The Yoga Matrix.* Louisville, Colo.: Sounds True.

Hahn, Thich Nhat. *The Art of Mindful Living.* Louisville, Colo.: Sounds True.